...stard ...
...ntil ...
...iff ...
...dd ...

## Never Fail Cake

...dients :- ½ cup butter. 1 cup sugar, 1½ cups
self raising flour. ¾ cup milk 2 eggs
pinch salt. essence.

...thad :- Beat butter & sugar to a cream, add
...ll beaten eggs, then beat in about 2
...blespoons flour, then add milk, stir, then
...dd remainder of flour. This mixture can
... divided into two cakes, add cochineal
...cup of cocoanut to one half. Leave th...
...her plain. Cook in moderate oven 20 to 25 m...

## Rainbow Cake :

...ream 1 cup butter & 2 cups sugar then ... th...
...eggs one at a time & beat well, then still...
...all cup milk, lastly add 3 cups fl...
...ll with 1 teaspoon e...
...boons cream of akis Plu...
... one le...
... flakis ... milk for about
... one large cup of bread...

*Our family table*

# JULIE GOODWIN

*My nan, Edna White, holding my mum*

'My friends are my family,
and my family are my friends.'

Margaret Fulton

*Mick's grandma, Imelda
Henebery, serving one of her
famous sponge cakes*

# Our *family* table

# JULIE GOODWIN

*Australia's first MasterChef*

EBURY
PRESS

For my boys,

Mick,

Joe, Tom and Paddy,

with love, gratitude and awe

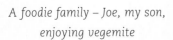

My favourite photo

A foodie family – Joe, my son,
enjoying vegemite

# Contents

*Nan, sitting in front of a caravan that Pop built*

# Author's note

Throughout this book I often recommend that you use a chef's pan. This is similar to a frying pan, only larger and heavier, with straight deep sides. My pan is 32 cm across and 7.5 cm deep with a non-stick surface and an ovenproof handle. It's a piece of equipment I use almost daily and I would suggest investing in one if you can.

Unless stated otherwise, all butter is unsalted. (This allows you to add seasoning to taste, rather than being stuck with the amount of salt in the butter.)

Eggs are large (59 g) and free-range.

When I refer to shallots, I am talking about the long green onions that are sometimes called spring onions or eschallots. When I refer to brown shallots, I am talking about those that look like daffodil bulbs or small brown onions. These are also known as French shallots.

*Grandma, stepping out with two cakes and a smile!*

# Foreword

It was gripping television. Each week, millions of viewers watched entranced as the gaggle of keen amateur cooks faced cameras, judges and talented, demanding chefs, competing for the prestigious title of *MasterChef*.

Julie Goodwin was a favourite from the start. Julie left no doubt that she loved to cook and was happiest when cooking food for family and friends, but she was keen to try out new skills. Julie worked hard at making her dishes taste good and soon showed a flair for plating and presenting them in a professional way. Learning from her successes (and mistakes), we witnessed her sheer pleasure in preparing food for the judges, and her final triumph – winning the *MasterChef* title.

It was natural that Julie should write a book about her love of cooking. Her enthusiasm and magic come through as she encourages us to cook together, with our families and our children. She urges us to enjoy cooking – to touch, to smell and, above all, to taste as you go! She reminds us that mealtime is a time not only to nourish ourselves and others, but to communicate and share the day. No matter how simple the meal, we should create a special place and sit down together at a carefully set table.

The desire to eat good food in good company is basic. There is pleasure in thinking about food – what to have for dinner, that next party, the next celebration; reading recipes and books; imagining tastes and combinations of flavours. This book is for everyone who loves food, loves to cook, or wants to learn to cook.

Congratulations, Julie, you are an inspiration.

*Margaret Fulton*

# Introduction

Life can certainly take some interesting twists and turns. This time last year, I was planning our family Christmas and looking forward to a couple of weeks by the beach afterwards. I had filled in an online application form for a cooking competition called *MasterChef*, and then forgotten all about it.

In January, I received a phone call to say I had been granted an audition for the show. In February I competed in the top 50 and made it to the finals. In March, I moved into a mansion with nineteen strangers, not knowing that I wouldn't return home for more than four months – and that when I eventually returned, it would be to a profoundly changed life.

Since *MasterChef*, I have been asked hundreds of times what started me cooking, and why I love it so much. As a child, I was taught the basics by Mum and have fond memories of learning to cook pikelets at her side when I was very little. I wasn't given my head too often in the kitchen, though, as I tended to be extremely messy.

When I left home and had my own family, and my own kitchen to mess up, I really started to get into cooking – experimenting, trying to recreate things I had tasted and enjoyed elsewhere, swapping recipes and ideas with my friends. And I learned a fundamental truth about human beings, a truth understood by generations of cooks before me: if you make nice food for people, they love you.

And so I began to realise that being able to cook well meant more than just being able to eat well. I noticed just how pivotal the food was at any gathering, how any celebration or get-together revolved around the dishes served. I began to really observe the kinship that occurs naturally over a shared meal.

I also learned that when I cook with time, and patience, and love, the food tastes so much better than when it is rushed. This lesson came home to me in a very real way during my time in the *MasterChef* kitchen. When I was panicky or fearful, my food reflected my state of mind. I realised that I had to find that serene place within, the calm that cooking brings me, even in the midst of all that chaos. I had to draw on that and bring it to the table. It was only when I understood this that I was able to bring my best effort forward to be judged.

Winning the competition, and in particular being granted the opportunity to write a cookbook, is in every sense a dream come true. It is an opportunity for me not only to record the recipes that my own family loves to eat, but to draw on the diversity and creativity of the people who surround me. Generations ago, extended families tended to live closer together and could count on one another for babysitting, meals, help about the house and garden, whatever was needed. These days we are often far-flung from our families. Although technology has given us connections to people half a world away, we still need to be connected in a real and touchable way to people nearby. This is where friends and community step in and fill what is often a gap in people's lives.

There are so many books available that explore the cutting edge of the food industry: new ingredients, new techniques, new methods of presentation. They are wonderful to read and experiment with. I have many of this type of cookbook and have learned a lot from them – but this book does not explore the new. Rather it is a simple cookbook with simple recipes, a wander through the world of the old and familiar with my family and my friends. It's a revisitation of food and ingredients that have brought comfort in the past. It is a peek into the food memories of others, an opportunity to compare and to remember for ourselves the things that brought us pleasure. Throughout *Our Family Table* you will find stories that all relate, in one way or another, to food. To how food is prepared, or shared, or what it has meant in the lives of the contributors.

The joy that we all found in recalling these stories was a gift in itself. We laughed and cried as long-forgotten tales were dusted off and brought out. Perhaps in remembering the things that made us happy as children we may resurrect some old recipes or rituals for our own children – or even create new ones.

During the writing of *Our Family Table*, we laid to rest my beautiful grandmother, Edna White, and also my far-too-young mother-in-law, Kathleen Goodwin. These losses brought home to me how important it is to talk while we have the chance, to record memories and collate photos and collect old letters and recipes and stories while we still can. So much of what we know is stored only in our minds and is easily lost.

My heartfelt thanks go out to all of the contributors. Reliving the many wonderful moments of our past – the camping, the Christmas feasts, the laughter – has made me so grateful to my mum, Marlene, and dad, Tony. Along with my amazing sister, Debbie, her partner, Kieron, and their gorgeous children, I know we will all continue to celebrate life in a way that always made Nan proud and will continue to do so.

Mick's family was a free-flowing stream of stories about his mum, Kathleen, and his grandma Imelda. Thanks to Mick's siblings, Paul, Liz, Rebecca, Anthony and Ben, and their wonderful partners, Lyn, Steve and Andrea, and all their beautiful children. Mick's uncles, aunts and cousins have also been very forthcoming with their recollections and advice – particularly the Henebery males on the subject of camp cooking and barbecuing. Thanks to Brian, the Photo Finder and Tong Master, as well as Vince, Saul, Andrew, Carmel and Sarah, and Rosemary, the Keeper of the Archive. For all of Mick's family, remembering the past has been joyful but also difficult, in this year of losing Kathleen, beautiful mum, grandmother and beloved sister. I am grateful for their sharing and hope that the book serves in some small way to keep the many good memories alive.

The diversity of culture among our friends is a source of inspiration to all of us as cooks. From Helene's Sri Lankan feast to Megan's Dutch treats and Kylie's Italian delicacies, I love the feeling of bringing not only friends but cultures together around the table. I am grateful to Mary, Natasha, Steph, Daniel, Adam, Vickie, Wayne and

Elizabeth; Louise and her mum, Jan, and their mate, Thelma; and friends of my parents, Cheryl and Gabrielle – all dear friends with an abundance of their own stories, memories and recipes.

Inspiration even flowed from the workplace, with contributions from Rose, Anthony, Leon, Josh, Kyle and Marcus from the team at Loyal I.T. Solutions.

As promised, the last chapter in this book has been left blank. I sincerely hope that you will begin your own collection of stories, recipes, pictures, words and memories. As important as the material itself, is the gathering of it – the sharing. My hope for this book is that you the reader will use the recipes to create delicious food for the people you love. I hope it draws you into the kitchen, and that you enjoy what you cook. But more importantly, I hope it encourages you to start a dialogue with the people in your own life about food and celebrations and the role they have played in your personal history. I hope it sets you on a journey of your own.

Most importantly of all, I hope that it inspires the creation of new memories. I hope it encourages the celebration of community through the sharing of a meal with others. I hope that, just like in generations past, the gift of a meal can bring peace or relief or happiness to someone in need.

It's a big ask for a little book, but these days I have every reason to believe in dreams coming true.

*Julie Goodwin, 2010*

*Mum and Uncle Barry on a camping holiday, with their catch*

# 1 | Good morning

I remember walking down the street one Sunday morning some years ago, with the double stroller and a toddler at my side, and passing an open-air cafe. There were all these people sitting serenely, sipping coffee, having polite conversations, eating cooked breakfasts and reading the paper in the sun. I recall looking at them with such envy and wishing for the day when the boys would be big enough for Mick and me to enjoy such a leisurely and civilised breakfast.

Now, I sit in cafes myself and watch people go by with their strollers, and I still feel a pang of envy. I am reminded of how quickly that special time flew by, and wish I hadn't wished a moment of it away.

Any weekend when we have nothing on is a special occasion. Joe, who is thirteen, loves so much to get up before everyone else and cook breakfast. He will bring me a cup of tea in bed and then fill the house with the delicious smell of bacon and eggs cooking. He has practised enough now to get it right all by himself. Coming downstairs to a beautifully cooked breakfast, after a bit of a lie-in, is one of life's great pleasures.

We take every opportunity now to enjoy a weekend lie-in and a long breakfast with the newspaper. It was a longed-for luxury all those years ago and we're not about to wish these days away too.

# Buttermilk pancakes

## makes 8

Preparation time: 10 minutes
Cooking time: 3 minutes per pancake

In our family, pancakes go down very well. My sister Debbie was looking after
all seven of our children one weekend, and she made pancakes for them. The kids still
talk about the enormous number of pancakes they ate in one sitting. It is too embarrassingly
high a number for me to repeat here. Suffice to say Debbie stood at the stove for a very
long time making pancakes for the eating machines we call our children.

1 cup (150 g) self-raising flour
¼ tsp bicarbonate of soda
¼ cup (55 g) caster sugar
1¼ cups (310 ml) buttermilk
1 egg
olive oil cooking spray
sliced banana, to serve

**Caramel sauce**
125 g cold unsalted butter, cubed
½ cup (100 g) brown sugar
½ cup (125 ml) pouring cream

1   To make the caramel sauce, combine all the ingredients in a medium saucepan. Stir over
low heat until the butter melts and the sugar dissolves. Bring to the boil, then reduce the
heat and simmer, uncovered, for 5 minutes or until thickened. Set aside to cool slightly.

2   To make the pancakes, sift the flour and bicarbonate of soda into a bowl and stir in the
sugar. Make a well in the centre. Whisk the buttermilk and egg together and stir gently
into the flour mixture.

3   Heat a frying pan over medium-low heat and spray it with oil. Pour ¼ cup of batter into the
pan and swirl it around. Cook for 2 minutes or until bubbles form on the surface. Turn and
cook a further 1 minute, or until cooked through. Repeat with the remaining mixture, then
serve with the caramel sauce and sliced banana.

*'Pancakes with lemon and sugar was always
a weekend winner at my house.' – Daniel*

# White chocolate and raspberry muffins

## makes 6

.................................................

Preparation time: 10 minutes
Cooking time: 20–25 minutes

This is a very indulgent recipe, absolutely delicious, dense and moist. What I would call a 'sometimes food' for sure – but every now and again, with a very good coffee, lovely.

2 cups (300 g) self-raising flour
¾ cup (165 g) caster sugar
¾ cup (130 g) white chocolate bits
1½ cups (180 g) raspberries

2 eggs
½ cup (125 ml) vegetable oil
½ cup (125 ml) milk

1 Preheat the oven to 180°C (160°C fan-forced) and line a 6-hole 'Texas' muffin pan with paper cases. Combine the dry ingredients in a large bowl, then chop about half of the raspberries and mix both the whole and chopped berries with the dry ingredients. Make a well in the centre of the bowl.

2 Whisk the eggs, oil and milk together and pour onto the dry ingredients. Using a wooden spoon or spatula, gently stir the wet ingredients into the dry ingredients until just combined. Too much mixing at this stage will result in tough, chewy muffins, but you do need to ensure there are no lumps.

3 Spoon the mixture among the paper cases and bake for 20–25 minutes or until golden on top and springy to touch. Turn out of the muffin pan and serve warm to grateful recipients.

*Note*: You can use frozen berries in this recipe, but fresh in season . . . wow!

# Perfect poached eggs

Breaking into a perfectly poached egg is one of the most satisfying moments in life – but there does seem to be a lot of contention and anxiety around how best to cook them. Some people create a whirlpool in the pot; some people put vinegar in the water; some people wrap the eggs in cling wrap, or use electric egg cookers. I steered clear of doing it myself after a few attempts that ended in a watery, eggy soup. Not very satisfying at all.

So, I was quite nervous when I did work experience at a busy Sydney cafe and was put in charge of the egg section – including the poached eggs. My nerves soon disappeared, though, as the cafe had a poaching method so easy it makes me wonder how I ever used to muck it up. I have adapted their method to suit a home kitchen.

For a good result you should use the freshest eggs you can.

In a large non-stick chef's pan or deep frying pan, bring about 4 cm of water to the boil, then lower the heat so that the water is barely simmering.

Crack the first egg gently on the side of the pan and, as carefully as you can, lower it into the water. Then leave it alone! The egg will gather the bulk of its white to itself. Any stringy floaty bits can be ignored. If the eggs are really fresh, not too much will get away.

Repeat with the remaining eggs, but don't do more than four in a large pan at a time. The water may need to be strained or replaced every few batches.

When the white looks cooked through (it should take about 3 minutes), carefully lift out each egg with a slotted spoon. If the white is still translucent or wobbly, set it back in the water until it cooks. If you prefer your egg yolks to be firm (a preference I will never understand), leave them in the water until the yolk lightens in colour. After removing the eggs from the pan, rest the slotted spoon briefly on a paper towel to remove excess water, then slide them straight onto the serving plate.

# Eggs Benedict

## serves 2

Preparation time: 10 minutes
Cooking time: 5 minutes

My favourite breakfast of all time is eggs Benedict. I suspect that this is because it took me a very long time to master the art of poaching eggs, so whenever I ate breakfast out, I would order it. Strictly speaking, eggs Benedict is an English muffin topped with ham, poached eggs and hollandaise sauce. Substituting smoked salmon for the ham results in eggs Royale, and using spinach instead would be eggs Florentine. I like my eggs Benedict on buttered, toasted Turkish bread instead of the muffin. I don't know what that ought to be called, but I know it's delicious.

| | |
|---|---|
| 2 slices Turkish bread, toasted | 4 eggs, poached |
| soft butter, to spread | ½ cup (125 ml) hollandaise sauce (see overleaf) |
| 150 g leg ham, shredded | chopped parsley, to serve |

1   Lightly butter the toast and place it on two warm plates. Top with the ham and gently rest the poached eggs on top of this.

2   Spoon over the hollandaise sauce, then sprinkle with chopped parsley and serve immediately.

*Note*: If you are using smoked salmon instead of ham, replace the parsley with finely chopped dill.

*'It's my honour to make Mum's breakfast on Mother's Day. Bacon and eggs sunny side up because that makes her smile. Tom makes the coffee and Paddy makes the toast. Dad sets the tray. Mum loves it.' – Joe*

*'I like to make the coffee for Mum's breakfast in bed on Mother's Day. I make it in one of her nice teacups. It's the only day of the year I'm allowed to use Dad's coffee machine. I make great coffee.' – Tom*

# Hollandaise sauce

## makes about 1½ cups

Preparation time: 5 minutes
Cooking time: 15 minutes

Eggs are twice as good when they're slathered in this delicious golden sauce.

¼ cup (60 ml) white wine vinegar

3 egg yolks, at room temperature

175 g butter, melted and cooled
to room temperature

2 tbs lemon juice

salt and ground white pepper,
to taste

1   Combine the vinegar with ¼ cup of water in a small saucepan. Bring to the boil, reduce
the heat and simmer for about 2–3 minutes, or until reduced to just under 2 tablespoons.

2   Place a glass bowl over a pan of barely simmering water. The bowl should not touch the water.
Put the vinegar reduction in the bowl, add the egg yolks and whisk until they are pale, creamy
and thickened slightly.

3   Ladle in the butter a little bit at a time, whisking constantly. The sauce will gradually start
to thicken. This part of the process takes several minutes – be patient. Remove the bowl from
the heat and whisk in the lemon juice a few drops at a time until it has the right amount of zing.
Season with salt and pepper to taste.

*Note*: If the sauce splits, or looks grainy, remove the bowl immediately from the heat and sit it
in cold water. Put 1 tsp of lemon juice in a fresh bowl and whisk in a little bit of the split sauce
until they combine. Keep adding the remaining sauce a bit at a time until it's all incorporated.

*'I always give Mum the present I got from the Mother's Day stall,
and I make her a card. Mother's Day is like a big thank you because
our mum does stuff for us every day.' – Paddy*

*'When the boys were little it was hard to let them make the breakfast without interfering
too much. Jules got some pretty dodgy breakfasts in those early years. Now they make it all
by themselves and it's great. Joe makes better eggs than I do.' – Mick*

# Asparagus with poached eggs and hollandaise

## serves 2

Preparation time: 10 minutes
Cooking time: 5 minutes

In spring, asparagus is in season, inexpensive and gorgeous. Simply blanched, with poached eggs and hollandaise, it makes a real treat for breakfast or brunch.

1 bunch young asparagus    4 eggs, poached (see page 6)
2 slices prosciutto    ½ cup (125 ml) hollandaise sauce
(see page 8)

1   Bring a medium saucepan of salted water to the boil. Have a bowl of cold water ready nearby. Prepare the asparagus by removing the woody ends. This is best done by bending the spears at the cut end – they will snap in the right place.

2   When the water is boiling, plunge the asparagus in. The thickness of the spears will dictate how long the asparagus should remain in the water, but it is only for a few moments – say 30 seconds for thin spears and up to 2–3 minutes if they're thicker.

3   Remove the asparagus from the boiling water with a slotted spoon, then dunk it immediately but very briefly in the cold water. This will stop the cooking process and keep the asparagus a vibrant green colour. Remove it from the water, drain and pat dry with paper towels.

4   Cut the prosciutto in half lengthways and cook under a hot grill until crisp. Arrange the asparagus spears on a warm plate. Top with poached eggs and hollandaise sauce. Place the two prosciutto pieces across the top and serve immediately.

*'Pour yourself as much cereal as you want,
but what you pour, you eat.' – Kathleen*

# Very quick omelette

## serves 1

Preparation time: 5 minutes
Cooking time: 2 minutes

Cooked breakfast is usually a weekend treat, but if you like to start your day with a good hit of protein, this omelette can be made just as quickly as toast. For me, the key to getting omelettes right is finding a really good non-stick frying pan and doing it over and over again. Practice makes perfect! The method I use is easy, failsafe and versatile.

2 eggs

1 tbs thickened cream

½ tsp olive oil, or olive oil spray

generous handful of grated tasty cheese – about ¼ cup

salt and white pepper, to taste

1 Preheat a 20 cm heavy-based non-stick frying pan over medium-high heat. (On my gas cooktop, this means high heat on the smallest burner. On an electric cooktop, practise until you know what works.)

2 Break the eggs into a bowl, add the cream and beat with a fork. Don't over-beat the eggs – they just need to be combined. Heat the olive oil in the pan, or spray it lightly with oil.

3 Pour the egg mixture into the pan. Allow it to set for a few moments and then, using a spatula, push the mixture from the edge to the centre. Turn the pan from side to side to make sure the base is covered. Wait a few moments, then repeat. When there isn't enough runny egg to keep coating the base of the pan, stop agitating and let it set.

4 Use the spatula to go around the edges of the omelette and make sure they are tidy. Season with salt and pepper and throw a handful of cheese across it. Carefully lift one side of the omelette and check for colour – it should be a light golden brown. If it is, fold it in half, then slide it onto a plate. This whole process should only take 2 minutes.

*Note*: I would rarely, if ever, serve an omelette this plain. A few chopped herbs from the garden, a little crumbled feta or some seeded diced tomato can give a real lift. Cooked fillings might include bacon, mushrooms or asparagus – just cook the filling first and set it aside, then sprinkle it across half the omelette before folding the other half over the top.

# Dill omelette with smoked salmon and crème fraîche

## serves 2

Preparation time: 15 minutes
Cooking time: 4 minutes

Smoked salmon is a beautiful way to start the day. It brings a bit of luxury
to breakfast time. Of course, it is also wonderfully good for you!

| | |
|---|---|
| 4 eggs | 2 slices smoked salmon, cut into 3 strips |
| 2 tbs thickened cream | ½ tsp salmon roe (extravagant optional extra) |
| 1 tsp chopped fresh dill | a few dill sprigs, for presentation |
| salt and white pepper, to taste | toasted Turkish bread and lemon wedges, |
| 2 tsp crème fraîche | to serve |

1   Make an omelette following the recipe on page 12, omitting the cheese, and adding the chopped dill to the egg mixture.

2   Plate the omelette and then repeat with the remaining mixture to make another.

3   Top the omelettes with a dollop of crème fraîche, strips of smoked salmon and the salmon roe. Finish with dill sprigs and serve with toasted Turkish bread and lemon wedges.

*Note*: Apparently in a restaurant, the done thing is to ensure that no edges of the omelette are exposed. The omelette is folded in three, rather than just in half, and the edges are tucked underneath. There is a real art in folding them to perfection. Give it a go if it's a special breakfast. Otherwise, slide it on the plate and enjoy it while it's hot!

*'For Mother's Day I refuse breakfast in bed as I like to be with my family.
When the children were younger they always prepared breakfast while I turned
a blind eye and resisted the temptation to tell them how to do it.' – Elizabeth*

# Vegetarian frittata

## serves 4

Preparation time: 10 minutes
Cooking time: about 15 minutes

I love that this dish can be varied depending on what's in the fridge, or in season.
It's a great way to use zucchini when there's an overabundance in the vegie patch, and
it's also very nice with fresh corn kernels. It can just as easily be made a non-vegetarian
dish with the addition of some sautéed chorizo or bacon, and it's a lovely, simple brunch
dish with some crusty bread and salad.

| | |
|---|---|
| 1 tbs olive oil | ¼ cup (60 ml) cream |
| 1 red onion, diced (not a fine dice – about 1 cm) | ½ cup (60 g) grated tasty cheese |
| ½ red capsicum, diced into 1 cm pieces | salt and white pepper, to taste |
| 6 thin asparagus spears, trimmed and cut into 2 cm lengths | 12 cherry tomatoes, halved |
| | ½ cup (40 g) grated parmesan cheese |
| 6 eggs | handful of parsley leaves, to serve |

1   Heat the olive oil in a 26 cm non-stick frying pan with an ovenproof handle over medium-high
heat. Add the onion and capsicum and stir until they are beginning to soften, then add the
asparagus pieces.

2   Whisk the eggs and cream together in a bowl, then stir in the tasty cheese and season with salt
and pepper. Add the cherry tomatoes to the pan, then pour the egg mixture over and reduce the
heat to low. Stir for only a moment, to distribute the vegetables evenly around the base of the pan.

3   Cook until the egg is setting and has turned golden brown on the bottom (check by very carefully
lifting an edge with a silicone spatula). This should take around 3–4 minutes. Sprinkle the
parmesan cheese over the top and put the frying pan under a hot grill for another 3–4 minutes,
until the cheese is golden and bubbling and the frittata is set. Slide it out of the pan onto a board
or platter and cut into wedges. Serve straight away, sprinkled with vibrant fresh parsley.

*Note*: If your asparagus isn't thin enough, you could blanch it first, or cut it in half lengthways
into 2 cm pieces.

# Breakfast bruschetta with sautéed mushrooms

## serves 4

Preparation time: 10 minutes
Cooking time: 10 minutes

If there's a French breadstick in the house, a quick and lovely cooked breakfast
can be made with just about anything else in the fridge. Mushrooms are my favourite.
This recipe yields about 3 cups of cooked mushrooms, enough for several rounds of toast.
Roasted tomatoes or scrambled eggs are good too – see overleaf for more recipes.

| | |
|---|---|
| 1 French breadstick | 500 g button mushrooms, sliced |
| 50 g butter | salt and ground black pepper |
| 1 tsp olive oil | 2 tbs finely chopped parsley, to serve |

1 Diagonally cut a French breadstick into the required number of slices, about 1 cm thick,
and brush both sides with olive oil. Place under a hot grill, on a chargrill pan, or in a frying
pan, and cook until golden brown on each side.

2 Place the butter and olive oil in a large frying pan over high heat. When the butter is foaming,
add the mushrooms and cook, stirring frequently, until browned. There should be plenty of space
for the mushrooms or they will stew rather than frying and the result will be completely different.
When they are brown and soft, spoon them onto the hot toast slices. Season to taste and sprinkle
with parsley.

*'Mother's and Father's Day usually start with breakfast in bed,
consisting of cold crumpets or toast, or pancakes . . .
we all sit on the bed and eat and then open up gifts.' – Rose*

*'I love lying in bed on Mother's Day listening to the boys in the kitchen shushing
each other, whispering and giggling about their "secret surprise". Then they sit on
the bed and watch me eat what they have created, and they are so proud.' – Steph*

Good morning

# Roasted tomatoes

## serves 4

.........................................................................

Preparation time: 5 minutes
Cooking time: 40 minutes

Just as I talk to my butcher, I like to talk to my local greengrocers, too. I know what day they go to the market and therefore the best day to visit for the freshest produce. We're growing our own tomatoes at home but until we're more competent gardeners, I'll still be relying on the greengrocer for this recipe. For the most beautiful roasted tomatoes, choose very red ripe Romas.

4 Roma tomatoes
¼ cup (60 ml) olive oil
1 tsp sea salt
1 tsp sugar

½ tsp ground black pepper
½ tsp dried oregano
¼ cup basil leaves

1   Preheat the oven to 200°C (180°C fan-forced). Cut the tomatoes in half lengthways and place them on a baking tray lined with non-stick baking paper. Drizzle with olive oil.

2   Combine the salt, sugar, pepper and oregano, and sprinkle over the tomatoes. Place in the oven for around 40 minutes – the tomatoes will soften and collapse. Serve on toast slices topped with shredded basil.

*'My favourite lazy breakfast is bacon, eggs and tomato.*
*I would eat it every day.' – Marcus*

# Scrambled eggs and feta

## serves 4

Preparation time: 5 minutes
Cooking time: 5 minutes

The feta in this recipe gives the eggs a lovely saltiness, so seasoning
is probably not required – but that's up to you!

| | |
|---|---|
| 4 eggs | 100 g good-quality feta, diced |
| 2 tbs cream | 1 tbs chopped fresh oregano leaves |
| 50 g cold butter, cubed | |

1   Whisk the eggs gently with the cream. Add the cold cubed butter to a frying pan over low heat and pour in the egg mixture. (This needs to be done over a low heat so the eggs will set without browning.) When the eggs start to set on the bottom of the pan, scatter the feta over the top.

2   Gently run a spatula across the bottom of the pan and around the sides, in effect turning the mixture upside down. Repeat this process until the eggs are done to your liking. Try not to agitate the eggs too much and don't cook them until they're completely dried out or they will be rubbery instead of soft.

3   Scatter with oregano and serve on toast slices.

# Corn fritters with bacon and tomato relish

## serves 4 (makes about 12)

Preparation time: 15 minutes + 15 minutes resting
Cooking time: about 3 minutes per batch

Corn fritters are not only a great brunch dish, they also go well with grilled chicken breast and avocado for an easy weeknight dinner.

3 cobs fresh corn, silk and husk removed
2 eggs, whisked
⅓ cup (80 ml) milk
¾ cup (115 g) self-raising flour
3 shallots, finely sliced

¼ cup chopped coriander leaves
salt and white pepper, to taste
olive oil for frying
8 rashers bacon, cooked to your liking
tomato relish, to serve (see page 163, or use your favourite bottled variety)

1   Cook the corn cobs either by boiling or microwaving them until the kernels are tender but still al dente. (Boiling will take about 5 minutes; if you're using a microwave, give it 1½ minutes per cob and then longer if required.) When the corn is cool enough to handle, run a sharp knife down the length of the cobs to remove the kernels.

2   Lightly beat the eggs and milk with a fork. Place the flour in a bowl and add the milk mixture gradually, stirring to ensure there are no lumps. Stir in the corn kernels, shallots and coriander. Season with salt and pepper and set aside for 15 minutes to rest.

3   Heat a thin layer of olive oil in a chef's pan or non-stick frying pan over medium heat. Drop heaped tablespoons of the mixture into the pan. Give the fritters space to spread and yourself space to flip them. After about 2 minutes they should be golden brown underneath. Flip and cook for another minute. Serve the fritters with the bacon and a generous dollop of tomato relish.

*Note*: You can pan-fry the bacon for this dish, then set it aside to keep warm. Keep the fat from the bacon and add it to the oil for frying the fritters. For a crispier result, cook the bacon under a hot grill.

# Potato rosti

## makes 8–10

Preparation time: 15 minutes
Cooking time: about 6 minutes per batch

These lovely potato cakes are traditionally served with smoked salmon, but they go just as well with fried eggs and bacon, or your favourite hot breakfast. Some recipes use eggs to bind the mixture, but if the potato is drained well and not rinsed (which removes the starch), they will stay together. They can be varied with the addition of chopped onion or herbs before cooking.

8 large potatoes (desiree, coliban or a similar waxy variety)
vegetable or canola oil, for shallow-frying

salt and freshly ground black pepper, to taste

1   Peel the potatoes and grate them into a colander. Take handfuls of the potato and wring out the excess moisture over the sink or a bowl.

2   Heat about 5 mm of oil in a large frying pan over a medium heat. The oil needs to be hot enough to produce a crisp golden shell without burning, while allowing the inside of the rosti to cook.

3   Place about three ½ cups of the potato mixture in the frying pan. Use a spatula or egg flip to flatten the potato into discs about 8–10 cm around. Fry for about 3 minutes on each side, until golden brown and crispy. Drain on paper towels and repeat until all the mixture has been used.

*'Perfect Sunday breakfast – eggs on toast with the yolks still runny, salty butter on the toast, coffee and the Sunday papers.' – Steph*

# 2 | Feeding the multitudes

This chapter is probably my favourite. It contains the food I serve to my family – dishes that have been cooked with love and received with gratitude over and over again – but it's also the kind of food that's shared with others, delivered with care and concern to neighbours and friends who are in need of a boost.

It is endlessly fascinating to me how we use food to say things we would otherwise struggle to say. Things like 'I would do anything to take your illness away but I can't – please accept this meal as something I can actually do to feel useful in the face of what's happening.' Things like 'I can't give you a good night's sleep and I can't be there to comfort your new baby at 3 am, but I can give you dinner and hope it takes pressure off you for a small part of your day.' Or 'I don't know you very well but I want to welcome you to the area.' Or simply, 'You deserve the night off.'

I was unexpectedly hospitalised a few years ago, just for a few days, when the three boys were very little. During this time enough food was delivered to the house to last for a week. It came from friends and family and community members. It helped Mick through the days I was away and allowed me to focus on getting well. 'It meant much more to me than "Here is some food,"' Mick said. 'It meant, "We love you, we are here for you, we support you."'

Offering the hand of friendship through a simple meal is a gesture that inspires in both the giver and the receiver a spark of kinship. In my ideal world, generosity would outweigh fear of scarcity; loneliness and hunger would not exist; and everyone would share a sense of belonging to something bigger than themselves. Perhaps that's a vision that won't come to pass in my lifetime. Perhaps it shows me up as naive, or a cockeyed optimist, or just woefully unrealistic. What I do know is that each of us has it in our power to take small steps towards our own ideal vision of the world. And it doesn't take a huge amount of time, or money, or even effort.

Next time you cook something, cook a double batch and sling some over the fence to your next-door neighbour. See what happens.

# Spaggy bol

## serves 6–8

Preparation time: 15 minutes
Cooking time: 4–5 hours in a slow cooker or 2 hours on the stovetop

With apologies to Kylie's Nanny Gina and others in the Italian community,
here is my very basic bolognese sauce. It's a family staple. I make it in double batches
and freeze some – it freezes very well and I think is even better the second time around.

| | |
|---|---|
| 1 tbs olive oil | 2 × 810 g tins crushed tomatoes |
| 2 onions, chopped | 2 tbs sugar |
| 2 garlic cloves, crushed | 1 tsp salt |
| 1 kg beef mince | cooked spaghetti, to serve |

1   Heat the olive oil in a chef's pan or large deep non-stick frying pan over medium heat. Add the onion and garlic and stir until soft but not brown. Add the mince to the pan and cook until brown. Use a wooden spoon to break up lumps in the mince.

2   If you have a slow cooker, put the mince mixture in, along with the tomatoes, sugar and salt. Simmer, covered, on the high setting for 2 hours, then uncover and cook for a further 2–3 hours, stirring occasionally.

3   To cook on the stovetop is equally effective but you need to be a lot more vigilant to make sure it doesn't burn on the bottom of the pot. Add the tomatoes, sugar and salt to the mince mixture. Keep it over a very low heat, uncovered, and stir it frequently for around 2 hours.

4   The sauce initially appears quite runny and pale. As it cooks and reduces, it achieves a thick consistency and a beautiful red colour. You will know when it's ready – it becomes very aromatic. Serve with dried spaghetti, cooked to packet instructions.

*'I was delivered a spag bol when I got home from having my baby. It was a nice surprise and took the burden off me for the evening. I felt loved.' – Mary*

# Ridiculously cheesy lasagne

## makes 1 family-sized lasagne

Preparation time: 15 minutes
Cooking time: 1 hour

This is the lasagne that won Mick over many years ago. It's hearty, rustic, big on flavour and would probably have Italian cooks throwing their hands in the air at my terrible disregard for authenticity.

Since learning how to make fresh pasta I love to use it in this recipe, but if you don't want to make your own, go for dried instant lasagne sheets instead. (A couple of 250 g packets should be enough.) Shop-bought fresh lasagne sheets seem to give inconsistent results, but I've used dried sheets to make this dish many times and, although it's different, it is still gorgeous.

1 quantity bolognese sauce (see page 28)   1 quantity cheese sauce (see page 33)
1 quantity fresh pasta dough (see page 32),   250 g grated tasty cheese
rolled out into lasagne sheets

1   Preheat the oven to 180°C (160°C fan-forced). Ladle a little bolognese sauce over the base of a 4 litre capacity baking dish (roughly 35 × 25 cm, and 6 cm deep). There needs to be enough sauce to cover the base, but keep it a thin layer (about 5 mm). Over this, lay the lasagne sheets.

2   Ladle half the bolognese sauce over the pasta, then ladle one-third of the cheese sauce on top. Carefully spread the cheese sauce to cover the meat. Scatter one-third of the grated cheese over this. Place another layer of pasta on top and repeat the bolognese and cheese sauces, then scatter over another handful of cheese.

3   Arrange the final layer of pasta, then ladle the remaining cheese sauce over the top. Generously cover this with the rest of the cheese. Cover with foil and bake for 45 minutes, then uncover and cook a further 15 minutes or until golden brown and bubbling on top. I like to serve this lasagne with parmesan cheese, a salad of mixed greens and garlic bread.

*Note*: This dish reheats beautifully. You can also cut the cooled lasagne into portions and wrap them individually in foil to freeze. Thaw them overnight in the fridge before reheating.

*'Look after your marriage first. If you have a happy marriage, you have a happy life.' – Grandma*

# Basic pasta dough

## makes enough for 4 bowls of spaghetti or 1 huge lasagne

Preparation time: 15 minutes
Cooking time: 2–3 minutes

Making fresh pasta is fun. It is tactile and messy and just the right thing to do with children. It definitely helps to have another pair of hands to hold the pasta and move it along the bench as you roll it out of the pasta machine. Make sure you keep the pasta and the work surface well floured.

| | |
|---|---|
| 200 g plain flour | 1 tsp olive oil |
| 2 eggs | ¼ tsp salt |
| 1 egg yolk | |

1 Place all the ingredients into a food processor and, using the pulse button, process in short bursts to a fine breadcrumb consistency.

2 Turn out onto a floured benchtop and gather into a ball. Knead well for several minutes. (This can also be done in a food processor with the right attachments, or an electric mixer with a dough hook, but bashing the dough around can be quite therapeutic.) The dough is kneaded enough when it is stretchy and smooth. Wrap it in cling wrap and put it in the fridge for around 15 minutes.

3 Prepare your benchtop for rolling out the pasta – make sure you have plenty of space and some plain flour handy. Work with half the pasta dough at a time. Roll it out until it is thin enough to be fed into a pasta machine. Feed the pasta through the thickest setting on the machine twice, then drop it a couple of settings. Feed it through twice again. Repeat until you are on perhaps the third-thinnest setting.

4 Take the long strip of pasta and fold the two ends into the middle. Fold in half. Repeat this process until the pasta is folded into a square. Turn the square 90 degrees, so it will travel through the pasta machine in the opposite direction to the last time, and feed it through the settings once again.

5 Repeat this whole process once more. On the last feed through the pasta machine, use the setting that is right for the pasta you are making. (My pasta machine's finest setting is extremely thin – I haven't used it yet.) Once the pasta is rolled, add the cutting attachment if required and cut the dough to the desired width.

*Note*: Fresh pasta cooks very quickly. Bring a big pot of salted water to the boil and cook for 2–3 minutes. When cooked, the pasta should be al dente – soft, but with a little bit of resistance to the bite.

# Cheese sauce

## makes 4 cups

Preparation time: 5 minutes
Cooking time: 15 minutes

If you have a good cheese sauce in your repertoire, you have loads of meals
at your fingertips – not just the cauliflower cheese and lasagne in this book, but
also dishes from a simple tuna bake right through to a lovely lobster mornay.
My boys adore it poured over hot pasta for a 'budgetarian' dinner.

| | |
|---|---|
| 50 g unsalted butter | 1 tbs Dijon mustard |
| ⅓ cup (50 g) plain flour | 200 g tasty cheese, grated |
| 3½ cups (875 ml) milk | salt and white pepper, to taste |

1   Melt the butter in a large heavy-based saucepan over medium heat. Add the flour and stir
constantly with a wooden spoon until it gathers into a dough (this is called a roux).
Continue to stir for another minute or two, as the flour begins to cook.

2   Add a little milk – about ¼ cup (60 ml). This will be incorporated into the roux fairly quickly,
and it will once again come away from the sides of the pan. Once this happens you can add another
¼ cup (60 ml) of milk and repeat until all the milk has been added and the mixture is smooth.
Cook, stirring occasionally so it doesn't catch on the bottom, until the sauce just comes to the
boil and thickens. Stir in the mustard, then add the cheese and stir until it melts. Taste and
season with salt and white pepper.

*Note*: To use this sauce for my cauliflower cheese recipe on page 60, simply halve the quantities.
Half of ⅓ cup is 2 level tablespoons. Or make the lot and keep some in the fridge for 3–4 days.

*'My best childhood food memory is Dad's hamburgers. He loved making and cooking
these for us. He used to chop raw onion and put it through the tomato sauce.
Dad's burgers had the lot – egg, pineapple, beetroot and of course his onion sauce.
Yum!' – Natasha*

# Nanny Gina's meatballs

## makes about 40

Preparation time: 20 minutes
Cooking time: 10 minutes per batch

My friend Kylie is from an Italian background, and her Nanny Gina is a legend in the family for her amazing, flavoursome and generous dishes. Here Nanny Gina shares her meatball recipe, which is always a part of the feast when the family comes around. Kylie swears that they have all tried to make meatballs just like Nanny's but they are somehow just never the same.

| | |
|---|---|
| 750 g pork mince | 1 large garlic clove, crushed |
| 250 g premium beef mince | 1½ cups (60 g) fresh breadcrumbs |
| 4 eggs | ⅓ cup chopped parsley |
| 3 fistfuls of grated cheese (about 1 cup), | salt and freshly ground black pepper |
| half parmesan and half pecorino | vegetable oil, for frying |

1   Combine all the ingredients except the oil in a large bowl and use your hands to mix them thoroughly. With damp hands, roll the mixture into meatballs about the size of a golf ball, keeping the size uniform. (You can make the meatballs larger or smaller if you prefer – but adjust the cooking time if you do.) Place on a plate and refrigerate for at least 30 minutes before cooking.

2   Heat about 3 mm of oil in a large frying pan and cook the meatballs over medium-high heat for about 10 minutes, shaking the pan occasionally, until they are well browned and cooked through. You will probably need to cook them in two batches, or in two frying pans at the same time, so you don't overcrowd your pan.

*Note*: If you want to serve these meatballs in a spaghetti sauce, add them to the sauce raw and simmer for about an hour. Garnish with basil leaves.

*'Sunday was supposed to be Mum's night off cooking, so we often had toasted sandwiches. Unfortunately for Mum, she was the one who made the toasted sandwiches. With eight of us in the house and only one sandwich maker, her night off was probably harder work than usual nights.' – Rebecca*

# Chicken parmigiana

## serves 4

Preparation time: 15 minutes
Cooking time: about 20 minutes

Although this dish can be seen sitting sadly in bains-marie across the country,
it really is at its absolute best when it's served straight after being cooked –
hot, crispy, bubbling with rich tomato sauce and golden cheese.

| | |
|---|---|
| 2 tsp olive oil | 4 single chicken breasts (small) |
| 1 onion, chopped | 1 cup (150 g) plain flour |
| 2 garlic cloves, crushed | salt and white pepper |
| 800 g can chopped tomatoes | 2 eggs |
| 1 tbs sugar | 3 cups (120 g) fresh breadcrumbs |
| ½ tsp salt | vegetable oil for frying |
| ¼ cup chopped basil leaves | 1 cup (80 g) finely grated parmesan cheese |

1   Heat the oil in a medium saucepan and sauté the onion and garlic over medium heat until soft.
Add the tomatoes, sugar and salt. Bring to the boil, then reduce the heat slightly and simmer
for 20 minutes, until reduced to about two-thirds of its original volume. The sauce should be quite
thick. Taste it and add more salt if required. Remove from the heat and stir through the basil.

2   Meanwhile, cut the chicken breasts in half horizontally to make two equally thick pieces.
Place the flour in a shallow bowl and season with salt and pepper, then beat the eggs
in a second shallow bowl with 1 tbs water. Put the breadcrumbs into a third shallow bowl.

3   Line up the flour, egg and breadcrumb bowls in a row. Dip each piece of chicken into the flour,
then the egg, then the breadcrumbs, shaking off the excess.

4   Heat 5 mm oil in a large frying pan or chef's pan over medium heat. Fry the chicken pieces
in batches – don't overcrowd the pan. Cook for about 3 minutes each side, by which time they
will be golden brown and cooked through but still juicy inside. If the heat is too high they will
colour too quickly and not be cooked enough in the middle. Use fresh oil after each batch to
avoid loose breadcrumbs burning and sticking to the fillets.

5   Preheat a grill to hot and arrange the chicken on a baking tray. Spoon the tomato sauce over
the top, then sprinkle with a generous handful of parmesan cheese. Put the baking tray under
the grill for about a minute, or until the parmesan starts to turn golden. Serve piping hot
with steamed seasonal vegetables or salad, or as pictured, right, on a bed of soft polenta.

# Marinated chicken wings

## serves 6

Preparation time: 20 minutes + marinating time (1 hour to 1 day)
Cooking time: 50 minutes

Not a dish that can be eaten elegantly – it's time for sticky fingers and messy faces.
It's wise to prepare plenty of these as they tend to get eaten! If you buy whole wings, joint them
into their three pieces with a sharp knife and keep the wingtips in the freezer for making
stock another day – but if you can buy the chicken wings already jointed, that's easier.
Try to get coriander bunches with decent-sized roots on them for this recipe.

½ cup (125 ml) hoisin sauce
½ cup (125 ml) soy sauce
¼ cup (60 ml) rice wine vinegar
3 garlic cloves, crushed
¼ cup (60 g) crushed ginger

¼ cup finely chopped coriander roots
2 kg chicken wings, jointed
¼ cup (60 ml) peanut oil
½ cup coriander leaves
¼ cup (40 g) chopped peanuts

1   Combine the hoisin, soy, rice wine vinegar, garlic, ginger and coriander roots in a bowl.
    Add the chicken wings and turn them to coat. Marinate in the fridge, covered, for at least
    an hour, but preferably overnight for full flavour.

2   Preheat the oven to 180°C (160°C fan-forced). Drain the chicken wings, reserving the marinade,
    then put them in a large baking dish and drizzle them with peanut oil.

3   Bake the chicken wings for 50 minutes or until dark brown and sticky. Meanwhile, place
    the reserved marinade in a saucepan with 1 cup (250 ml) water. Bring to the boil, then reduce
    the heat slightly and cook for about 15 minutes, or until the sauce reduces and thickens.

4   Serve the chicken wings with the sauce poured over them, topped with coriander leaves and
    chopped peanuts.

*Note*: This dish is pictured on page 78 with Asian greens. It is ideal served with rice.

*'Cook for an army in quantity, and hope there's some left over.' – Cheryl*

# Fish and chips

## serves 4

Preparation time: 30 minutes
Cooking time: about 30 minutes

Who doesn't love fish and chips? It evokes days at the beach – sunburned, sandy
and tired from swimming. Cooking it at home means you don't have to contend with hungry
seagulls, but it's not quite the same unless it's wrapped in paper and eaten with your fingers.

vegetable oil, for deep-frying
1 kg pontiac potatoes
salt, to taste
1⅓ cups (200 g) plain flour
375 ml cold beer
2 tsp salt

½ cup (75 g) plain flour, extra
salt and white pepper
8 × 100 g boneless white fish fillets
1 quantity tartare sauce (see overleaf)
lemon wedges, to serve

1   Preheat the oven to 100°C (80°C fan-forced). Fill a deep-fryer to the recommended
    level with clean vegetable oil and heat it to 160°C. Alternatively, half-fill a large pan and use a
    kitchen thermometer for temperature.

2   Peel the potatoes and cut them into 1 cm thick chips. Fry for about 8 minutes, or until they are a
    pale golden colour, then remove them from the oil and drain well in a colander.

3   Increase the temperature of the oil to 190°C, then fry the chips a second time, for 6–8 minutes,
    or until golden brown and crisp. Drain and sprinkle with salt, then place on an oven tray lined
    with non-stick baking paper to keep warm while you cook the fish.

4   Place the flour, beer and salt into a bowl and stir until combined. In a shallow dish, season the
    extra plain flour with salt and pepper. Coat the fillets in the flour, then carefully dip them into
    the batter. Allow the excess batter to drain, then lay each fillet gently and directly into the hot oil.
    (Don't put it into a basket and then lower it into the oil, as the batter will get stuck.) You should
    be able to put 3 or 4 fillets in the fryer at one time. Cook them for around 4 minutes, or until they
    are golden brown and crisp. Drain on paper towels and sprinkle with salt. Put the fish into the oven
    with the chips while waiting for further batches.

5   Serve hot and crunchy with tartare sauce and lemon wedges.

# Tartare sauce

## makes slightly more than 1 cup

Preparation time: 5 minutes
No cooking time

Better than anything you will find in a jar, and so easy to make – this will elevate your fish and chips to a gastronomic experience. For the best results, use my homemade mayonnaise (see page 158), or a good-quality whole egg mayonnaise.

1 cup (250 g) mayonnaise
2 tsp Dijon mustard
¼ cup (45 g) finely chopped capers

¼ cup (30 g) finely chopped dill pickles (gherkins)
2 tbs finely chopped dill

1   Combine the mayonnaise and Dijon mustard in a bowl.

2   Stir the chopped capers, pickles and dill through the mayonnaise mixture. Voila!

*'My job after tea was to wipe up while Dad washed. I loved this time with him and would talk nineteen to the dozen about my day and every other thought that popped into my head. Dad must have enjoyed the time with me too because he would keep washing the same clean dishes that I had already dried, two and sometimes three times, until I noticed I was wiping up the same things over and over again.' – Marlene*

# Crumbed cutlets

## serves 4

.......................................................................................................

Preparation time: 15 minutes
Cooking time: 20 minutes

When I was a kid, lamb was the cheap meat. Mince would have been a close second.
Steak was an extravagance rarely seen at our table. Things have changed a bit now.
Chicken seems to be the cheap meat, and lamb is up there with steak as a delicacy –
but every now and again, lamb cutlets are on special and I can indulge in one
of my favourite childhood dishes.

| | |
|---|---|
| 12 lamb cutlets | 2 eggs |
| ½ cup (75 g) plain flour | 2½ cups (100 g) fresh breadcrumbs |
| salt and freshly ground black pepper | ⅓ cup (85 ml) olive oil |

1   Using a meat mallet or rolling pin, gently hammer the lamb cutlets until they are just under
    1 cm thick. Combine the flour with salt and pepper in a shallow dish. Beat the eggs with
    ¼ cup (60 ml) water in a second shallow dish. Place the crumbs into a third shallow dish.

2   Set up the cutlets to the left of the other three dishes – it's about to be a production line. Dip
    the first cutlet in the flour and shake off the excess, bathe it in the egg mixture and then toss
    it in the breadcrumbs until it's generously coated. Place it on a clean plate, then repeat the
    process with the remaining cutlets.

3   Heat half the olive oil in a large heavy-based chef's pan or frying pan. Cook 4–6 cutlets at a time
    for 3–4 minutes each side or until golden brown and cooked to medium. Clean out the pan, add
    the remaining olive oil and cook the rest of the cutlets. Rest the cutlets for 5 minutes or so before
    serving, but no longer!

*'Dinner was always at 6.30 on the dot, straight after the news. We were
allowed one glass of milk. There was always dessert but we could
only have it if we cleaned our plate.' – Rebecca*

# Beef and broccoli stir-fry

## serves 4

Preparation time: 30 minutes + 1 hour marinating time
Cooking time: about 15 minutes

To make it easier to slice the beef thinly for this recipe, it can be put in the freezer until it has firmed up. As the meat is cooked very quickly, cheaper cuts of steak can be used. I specify rump because I love the flavour.

| | |
|---|---|
| 1½ tsp light soy sauce | 2 tsp cornflour, extra |
| 1½ tsp sugar | peanut oil, for stir-frying |
| 1 tbs cornflour | 6 shallots, cut into 3 cm lengths |
| 800 g lean rump steak, sliced thinly across the grain | 500 g broccoli, stalks thinly sliced, florets sliced |
| ¼ cup (60 ml) oyster sauce | 3 cloves garlic, crushed |
| 2 tbs light soy sauce, extra | ¼ tsp salt |
| 2 tbs dark soy sauce | ½ tsp sugar |
| | steamed rice, to serve |

1  Combine the light soy sauce, sugar and cornflour with 1 tbs water and mix well. It takes some work to integrate the cornflour into the other ingredients. Add the beef and toss well, ensuring it all gets a coating. Refrigerate, covered, for 1 hour.

2  Combine the oyster sauce, light and dark soy and 2 tbs water, then set aside. In a separate bowl, mix the extra cornflour with 2 tbs water.

3  Heat 2 tbs oil in a wok and, when hot, add about one-eighth of the sliced beef. Stir-fry until it is browned and almost cooked through, then remove it from the wok and drain on a paper towel. Repeat this process, cleaning out the wok with paper towel between each batch and setting the meat aside.

*Continued next page . . .*

Feeding the multitudes

Beef and broccoli stir-fry *continued...*

4   Heat 1 tsp oil in the wok. Briefly stir-fry the shallots until they are tender but still crisp, then set them aside with the meat.

5   Wipe out the wok with a paper towel again, then heat 2 tbs oil and add the broccoli pieces, garlic, salt and sugar. Stir-fry briefly, for 30 seconds or so. Add ½ cup (125 ml) water and cover for 3 minutes or until the broccoli is tender but crisp. It should remain a vivid green colour. Remove it from the wok and drain.

6   Wipe out the wok one last time and add 2 tbs oil. Return the broccoli, shallots and beef to the wok. Add the sauce ingredients and the cornflour mixture in a well at the bottom of the wok and stir until the sauce thickens. (For a spicier stir-fry, hot chilli sauce can be added at this final stage.) Toss to coat all the ingredients in the sauce and serve immediately on steamed rice.

*'Once Mum and my brother were both in the hospital at the same time. The church community and neighbours fed the rest of us for the whole time Mum was away. I remember the ladies coming with their meals, sometimes still with their oven mitts on, then staying to serve up to us.' – Rebecca*

*'I find in times of death, or an upheaval, delivering a meal to a friend is a way of saying, "Even if I can't make the situation different, I can try to make it easier."' – Rose*

# Helene's pork curry

## serves 6

Preparation time: 10 minutes
Cooking time: about 2 hours

My dear friend Helene is a magnificent Sri Lankan cook and this dish is a part of her traditional New Year's Day feast. My boys and I have had the privilege of enjoying this pork curry at Helene's place on several occasions. It is tender and tasty. Just the smell of the curry powder cooking gets our mouths watering every time.

| | |
|---|---|
| 1 kg pork (such as shoulder or scotch fillet) | 2 tsp chilli powder |
| 2 tbs vegetable oil | ¼ cup curry powder (see overleaf) |
| 1 large onion, chopped | 2 tsp salt |
| 4–5 garlic cloves, crushed | 1 tbs tamarind pulp |
| 1 tbs finely grated ginger | 1 tbs honey |
| 10 dried curry leaves | yoghurt and coriander leaves, to serve |

1   Cut the pork into bite-size cubes. Heat the oil in a large saucepan and fry the onion, garlic, ginger and curry leaves over medium heat for about 5 minutes, stirring often, until golden brown.

2   Mix the chilli powder, curry powder and salt with a little water to make a paste. Add the paste to the pan and continue to fry, stirring often, for about 2 minutes, until fragrant. Add the pork to the pan and stir to coat it thoroughly with the spice mixture.

3   Place the tamarind pulp in 1½ cups (375 ml) hot water, and squeeze it to extract the flavour. Pour the liquid over the pork and stir to combine.

4   Cover and bring to a simmer over low heat. Cook for 1½ hours, until the meat is very tender. Add the honey and cook uncovered for 15–20 minutes, or until the gravy thickens. Serve topped with yoghurt and coriander leaves.

*Note*: If you can't find tamarind pulp, you can use tamarind puree or tamarind concentrate, which are available from some large supermarkets and from Asian specialty shops. Puree and concentrate don't need to be squeezed – just add them to the water. If you don't want to make the curry powder, you can purchase ready-made Sri Lankan curry powder from a spice shop. Keep the remaining powder in an airtight container.

# Helene's curry powder

## makes about 1 cup

Preparation time: 5 minutes
Cooking time: 3 minutes

Even though Sri Lankan spice blends can be bought at the store, this is the way Helene makes it, and the way her mother and grandmother made it before her.

¼ cup (25 g) fennel seeds
2 tbs cumin seeds
½ cup (40 g) coriander seeds
1 tsp fenugreek seeds

2 handfuls dried curry leaves
5 cm cinnamon stick, broken up
5–6 cardamom pods (seeds only)

1  Combine the fennel, cumin, coriander and fenugreek seeds with the curry leaves in a large frying pan. Dry-fry over low heat for about 3 minutes, until fragrant and dark brown (not black!). Remember to keep stirring regularly so that the seeds won't burn.

2  Transfer to a bowl to cool, then place into a small food processor or spice grinder with the cinnamon and cardamom seeds. Blend to a fine powder and store in an airtight container.

*'We pray before the meal and bless the cook.' – Helene*

*'Dad passed away on a Thursday night. On Friday morning, Grandma (Mum's mum) turned up with her car boot loaded with food. There were biscuits, cakes and meals. She must have stayed up all night cooking. We ate for a week off that food.' – Rebecca*

# Veal with mushroom sauce

## serves 4

Preparation time: 15 minutes
Cooking time: about 20 minutes

This veal dish is beautiful accompanied by steamed vegetables.
The rich, creamy mushroom sauce is also lovely poured over steak or chicken.

| | |
|---|---|
| 4 large or 8 small veal schnitzels (800 g) | ½ cup (125 ml) white wine |
| 1 tbs olive oil | 2 tbs veal glaze or beef stock |
| 60 g butter | ½ cup (125 ml) thickened cream |
| 2 garlic cloves, crushed | 2 tsp Dijon mustard |
| 400 g button mushrooms, sliced | salt and white pepper, to taste |

1   Place the veal schnitzels between two sheets of cling wrap and beat them with a rolling pin until they're very thin. (If they're already paper-thin when you buy them, don't bother with this step.)

2   Heat the olive oil and 1 tbs of the butter in a chef's pan or large frying pan over high heat. Cook the veal quickly, only about 1 minute on each side, in batches so you don't overcrowd the pan. Set it aside on a plate and cover loosely with foil to keep warm.

3   Into the same pan, add the remaining butter and the garlic and mushrooms. Sauté until the mushrooms are browned. Deglaze the pan with the wine and simmer until it is almost evaporated. Add the stock, cream and mustard, then simmer until the sauce reduces slightly and starts to thicken. Season to taste, then pour over the veal. Sprinkle with ground black pepper, if you like.

*'Zac was in hospital with meningitis and I came home to find an entire, neatly wrapped roast chicken dinner on the doorstep, delivered to coincide with my arrival home from my "shift" at the hospital. It was the most meaningful demonstration of love and support that anyone showed us through those few terrible weeks. I was not raised to reach out to people in this way and it changed me. I realised that we were part of a community and we were not alone.' – Steph*

# 3 | A *bit* on the side

Sometimes the unsung heroes at the feast, side dishes can transport an ordinary meal and make it a memorable event. They range from the simplest of fresh steamed vegetables to fabulous combinations of colour, texture and flavour.

My favourite kind of entertaining involves a table laden with huge platters and bowls of fabulous food – roasted or grilled meat, pasta, casseroles, potatoes, salads and many incarnations of vegetables and sauces. There is bread and beer and wine and everyone helps themselves. Ideally there's enough for second and third helpings, and plenty left over for the next day.

When I was younger, all my nan's siblings and their families would meet at Putney Park once a year. We would spread out blankets by the Parramatta River, under the giant camphor laurel trees. Out of a dozen picnic baskets would come the most extraordinary feast. It varied from year to year, but certain staples were always present – loads of cold ham and chicken, potato salad, fresh bread with real butter, Aunty Joyce's cold meat pie and homemade fruitcake.

We would eat until we were fit to burst, then run it all off playing cricket. Uncle Sid would give all us kids a $2 note in a brown envelope and we felt like millionaires. And we might as well have been – how much richer can life get than enjoying a meal prepared by many and shared with love?

# Couscous with orange

## serves 4 as an accompaniment

Preparation time: 20 minutes
Cooking time: about 5 minutes

This salad can be a shared dish for a barbecue, or a lovely
accompaniment to lamb chops or grilled chicken.

¼ cup (35 g) currants

1 cup (250 ml) chicken or vegetable stock

1 cup (200 g) couscous

1 tbs butter

2 tsp olive oil

1 onion, chopped

2 garlic cloves, crushed

2 tsp curry powder

finely grated zest of 2 oranges

1 tbs brown sugar

1 orange, segmented (see note)

2 tbs orange juice

salt and pepper, to taste

1   Soak the currants in boiling water until they are plump – about 10 minutes.

2   While the currants are soaking, bring the stock to the boil in a covered saucepan over high heat.
Remove from the heat and add the couscous. Stir, then cover and leave for 5 minutes while the
couscous absorbs the liquid. Add the butter and fluff with a fork, then transfer to a large bowl.

3   Meanwhile, heat the oil in a non-stick frying pan over medium heat. Add the onion and cook,
stirring, for 2–3 minutes or until the onion softens. Add the garlic, curry powder and orange
zest and cook for a further minute. Stir through the brown sugar, then add the onion mixture
to the couscous.

4   Roughly chop the orange segments and stir them through the couscous, along with the drained
currants and the orange juice. Season to taste with salt and pepper.

*Note*: To segment an orange, use a small sharp knife and cut off all the skin, including the
white pith. Hold the orange in the palm of your hand and cut on either side of each segment,
inside the membrane. You should have neat segments of flesh with no pith or membrane.

*'Whoever cooks doesn't have to clean up. Usually.' – Mick*

# Creamy potato salad

## serves 6

Preparation time: 20 minutes
Cooking time: about 15 minutes

There's nothing worse than a bad potato salad – dry, or undercooked, or mushy. But there's almost nothing better than a good one. This is my version. The key is to cook the potatoes so that they're tender but not overdone, and then add plenty of delicious dressing.

600 g chat potatoes
½ cup (70 g) sour cream
½ cup (65 g) good-quality whole egg mayonnaise (homemade mayo is always best)
1 tbs wholegrain mustard
juice of ½ lemon
2 tbs chopped dill

2 tbs chopped basil
3 shallots, finely sliced
4 cooked bacon rashers, finely sliced (if desired)
salt and freshly ground black pepper
basil leaves, to garnish

1   Place the potatoes in a saucepan of cold water and bring them to the boil. Cook for about 15 minutes, until tender (the time will depend on their size). Drain and cool slightly.

2   Meanwhile, combine the sour cream, mayonnaise, mustard and lemon juice. Fold through the herbs and shallots, and the bacon, if you are using it.

3   Cut the warm potatoes into quarters if they're small, sixths if they're medium, and stir into the dressing. Season to taste.

*Note*: Choose potatoes of an even size, so they cook at the same time.

*'Pray – sing – take joy in everyday life.' – Grandma*

# Adam's favourite caesar salad

## makes a giant platter

......................................................................................................................

Preparation time: 15 minutes
Cooking time: 15 minutes

Regardless of what's in vogue and what isn't, some things just stay favourites.
My mate Adam always asks me to make my caesar salad when we go to their
place or they are coming to ours.

1 large cos lettuce

4 rashers bacon

6 slices bread, crusts removed, cubed

olive oil, to drizzle

salt, to taste

1 quantity Adam's favourite caesar
salad dressing (see overleaf)

1 red onion, finely sliced

4 eggs, boiled and sliced (I like it when the
yolk is still a little bit soft in the middle)

100 g parmesan cheese, shaved
with a potato peeler

1 Remove any shabby outer leaves from the lettuce and any leathery leaf tips. Cut the lettuce
crossways into 3–4 cm wide strips.

2 Remove the rind from the bacon and cut it into thin strips, then fry it in a large non-stick pan over
high heat until it begins to crisp up. Remove with a slotted spatula, and drain it on paper towels.

3 Reduce the heat to medium-low and add the bread cubes. Drizzle them with olive oil and toss them
around the pan until they are coated in the combined oil and bacon fat, then season lightly with salt.
Cook, tossing occasionally, until the bread is brown and crisp. Remove and drain on paper towels.

4 Just before serving, toss almost all of the dressing with the red onions and the lettuce.
Toss through the remaining dressing if you find you need it (this will depend on the size of your
lettuce). Arrange the lettuce and onion on a large flat platter and then top with the egg, bacon,
croutons and parmesan. Serve straight away.

# Adam's favourite caesar salad dressing
## makes about 1 cup

........................................................................................

Preparation time: 10 minutes
No cooking time

If I'm taking my caesar salad to Adam's place or anywhere else, I put all the separate components into zip-lock bags and put it together at the last minute. The dressing should be served at room temperature, as it hardens in the fridge.

| | |
|---|---|
| 1 tbs white wine vinegar | 1 egg yolk |
| 1 garlic clove, crushed | 1 cup (250 ml) light olive oil |
| 1 tbs Dijon mustard | lemon juice, to taste |
| 6 anchovy fillets, finely chopped | salt and white pepper, to taste |
| 1 tbs Worcestershire sauce | |

1   To make the dressing, combine the vinegar, garlic, mustard, anchovies, Worcestershire sauce and egg yolk in a large mixing bowl. Using electric beaters, beat until well combined.

2   Add the olive oil a few drops at a time, beating constantly, until the dressing starts to thicken. The oil can then be added in a stream. When the dressing is thick and smooth, add lemon juice, salt and white pepper to taste, and mix well.

*'One day Ken and I had been working in the yard all day levelling soil. When we were packing up our neighbour called me to the fence and handed over a beautiful lobster salad. It could have been a Vegemite sandwich and I would have appreciated it!' – Elizabeth*

# Cauliflower cheese

## serves 6 as an accompaniment

Preparation time: 10 minutes
Cooking time: about 20 minutes

This is one of those comfort foods that brings back memories of dinner at Nan's place. It's warm, it's cheesy, it's delicious – in fact, it would do me on its own for a winter lunch.

1 head cauliflower, cut into large florets     1 cup (125 g) grated tasty cheese
½ quantity cheese sauce (page 33)

1　Preheat the oven to 180°C (160°C fan-forced). Cover and cook the cauliflower for about 10 minutes on high in the microwave, or steam it for about 7 minutes, until tender.

2　Make sure any excess moisture is drained off and arrange the florets in a shallow 8 cup capacity casserole or baking dish. Try to keep the 'flower' side of the florets up where possible.

3　Pour the cheese sauce over the florets, making sure there are no gaps, and sprinkle with cheese. Bake uncovered for 10–15 minutes, or until golden brown on top.

*'As adults, my siblings and our partners would go to Mum and Dad's on a Thursday night for her lamb roast with homemade gravy, chicken, roast potatoes and pumpkin and cauliflower cheese. We finished with her famous apple pie with cream and ice-cream. I don't know how my mother did this every week, there were so many of us. It was chaotic, but always delicious and heart-warming.' – Mary*

# Mushrooms with speck

## serves 4

Preparation time: 10 minutes
Cooking time: 15 minutes

For this recipe it's best to choose the littlest, firmest button mushrooms you can.
If you can't get them small, buy larger ones and cut them in half. The rich flavour
of the mushrooms and speck, and the crunch of the bread, make this side dish lovely
in the cooler months, served alongside roasted red meat or casserole and potatoes.

3 slices stale bread, crusts removed
olive oil for sprinkling
salt, to taste
1 tbs olive oil, extra

200 g piece of speck or thick bacon,
cut into batons
250 g button mushrooms
2 tbs roughly chopped flat leaf parsley,
to serve

1  Preheat the oven to 150°C (130°C fan-forced), then shred the bread and arrange it on an oven tray.
The size of the bread pieces should be somewhere between a crouton and a coarse fresh breadcrumb.
Sprinkle them with olive oil and season with salt. Cook for 15 minutes, until crisp and lightly golden.

2  Meanwhile, heat the extra olive oil in a large frying pan over medium-high heat. Add the speck
and cook it for 2–3 minutes, until it is beginning to brown. Add the whole button mushrooms
and sauté for about 5 minutes, until golden and soft.

3  Serve topped with the baked bread and the parsley.

# Roast honey and sesame carrots

## serves 6 as an accompaniment

Preparation time: 10 minutes
Cooking time: 40 minutes

For years when I made baked dinners I steamed the carrots with a drizzle of honey.
And as yummy as that was, Mick approached me one day and asked, kind of sheepishly,
if I could bake them instead, like his mum did. I wondered if you could have too
many roast vegies in one dinner. The answer is no, and this dish is the result.

6 large, thick carrots (about 150 g each),
peeled and cut into thirds

30 g butter, cubed

2 tbs honey

2 tsp sesame seeds, toasted

1   Preheat the oven to 180°C (160°C fan-forced). Place the carrots in a small baking dish with
the butter and bake for 30 minutes, turning regularly, until they are soft and lightly browned.

2   Add the honey and toss well. Return the dish to the oven for a further 10 minutes or until
the honey turns golden brown and glazes the carrots.

3   Arrange the carrots on a platter and scatter them with sesame seeds to serve.

*Note*: To toast sesame seeds, place them in a dry frying pan and stir over medium heat
for 1–2 minutes, until they are golden. Transfer them to a plate to cool.

# Fresh creamed corn

## serves 4 as an accompaniment

Preparation time: 20 minutes
Cooking time: about 5 minutes

As a kid, creamed corn on toast was one of my favourite weekend breakfasts.
Of course, it was the tinned variety. Creamed corn made from fresh cobs is vibrant
and delicious, and goes perfectly with grilled chicken breasts or steak.

3 cobs corn
30 g butter
2 tbs cream
salt and white pepper

2 tbs finely chopped red capsicum
2 tbs chopped coriander leaves
1 tbs chopped shallot

1   Cook the corn cobs either by boiling or microwaving them until the kernels are tender but
    still al dente. (Boiling will take about 5 minutes; if you're using a microwave, give it 1½ minutes
    per cob and then longer if required.) When the corn is cool enough to handle, run a sharp knife
    down the length of the cobs to remove the kernels. Reserve ¼ cup of the whole kernels.

2   Put the remaining kernels into a food processor with the butter, cream, and salt and pepper to taste,
    then process until smooth.

3   Add the reserved whole kernels and the capsicum, coriander and shallot. Taste and adjust
    the seasoning, and reheat if necessary.

*'Best not to get on the phone while there's something on the stove. If you burn the pot,
soak it overnight. This usually means someone else gets to wash it up. If the pot is
really really badly burned, find a big bush to hide it in.' – Nan*

# Potato bake

## serves 8–10 as an accompaniment

Preparation time: 15 minutes
Cooking time: 1 hour 30 minutes

The simplicity of this dish makes it a great one to take to parties or to serve when you have a lot of people coming. It's equally at home at a special event, though, as it can be made in individual gratin dishes or sliced carefully and served with a romantic dinner for two. Quantities and cooking times would need to be adjusted accordingly.

2 kg potatoes
600 ml thickened cream
3 garlic cloves, crushed

1 tbs fresh thyme leaves
salt and white pepper, to taste

1 Preheat the oven to 180°C (160°C fan-forced). Peel the potatoes and slice them very thinly, using a sharp knife or a mandolin.

2 Combine the cream, garlic, thyme, salt and pepper in a large bowl. Toss the potatoes through until they are well coated.

3 Layer the potatoes in a large baking dish. (It doesn't matter what shape the dish is, but it should be around 6 cm deep and have a capacity of about 2.5 litres.) Arrange the top layer neatly, then press down on it firmly. Cover the dish with good-quality aluminium foil and press down again, so that the foil is touching the top layer of potatoes. Seal tightly on all sides, then bake for 1 hour. Remove the foil and cook for a further 30 minutes or until the top is brown and crisp.

*'If you are going to turn the oven on, cook more than one thing.' – Marlene*

# Rich potato puree

## serves 6–8 as an accompaniment

Preparation time: 10 minutes
Cooking time: about 10 minutes

This is definitely not your everyday mashed potato. It is so rich and buttery
that it really is a decadent, delicious treat for special occasions.

3 potatoes (around 700 g), peeled
1 cup (250 ml) milk

125 g good-quality unsalted butter, cubed,
at room temperature
salt, to taste

1   Halve the potatoes and place them in a large pan of cold salted water, then bring it to the boil.
Cook them until they're tender – about 10 minutes – and then strain them well. Empty the pan
and dry it, then return the potatoes to the pan.

2   Heat the milk in a separate saucepan, but don't let it boil. Using a potato masher, mash the potatoes
as quickly as possible, gradually introducing cubes of butter. Change to a sturdy wire whisk and
beat in the hot milk a little at a time until the puree is the consistency you want. For a thicker
puree, stop at ½ cup of milk; for a runny puree, stir in a full cup.

3   Taste the puree and add salt. (Be aware that potato tends to need quite a lot of salt in order not
to taste bland.) Keep whisking until the puree is completely smooth and free of lumps. For a truly
lump-free puree, push the mixture through a wire sieve with a spatula. As the potato cools it will
thicken up.

*Note*: To reheat any left-over puree, stir in a little extra milk over a gentle heat.

A bit on the side

# Not-very-authentic fried rice

## serves 8 as an accompaniment, 4 as a main

Preparation time: 20 minutes
Cooking time: 25 minutes

As the title indicates, this dish isn't very authentic. It can be varied in any number of ways, depending on what you have in the fridge and cupboard. With the addition of some prawns or marinated meat, it can be a meal on its own. I like my fried rice to be big on flavour, but if you prefer less salt or spice, adjust the soy sauce and five-spice to suit your taste.

2 cups (450 g) jasmine rice
4 rashers bacon, sliced thinly
½ cup (125 ml) peanut oil
1 brown onion, chopped
2 garlic cloves, crushed
2 tbs grated ginger
2 eggs

salt and white pepper
1 cup (150 g) frozen baby peas
1 tsp Chinese five-spice
⅔ cup (160 ml) soy sauce
6–8 shallots (depending on the size),
  thinly sliced diagonally
½ cup (35 g) crispy fried shallots

1   Place the rice together with 3 cups of water in a tightly lidded microwave-safe container with a capacity of about 2.5 litres. Cook on high for 18 minutes. When it's cooked, transfer the rice to a large wide bowl and fluff the grains with a fork.

2   Meanwhile, heat a wok or a large chef's pan and cook the bacon over medium heat for 2–3 minutes. Add 1 tbs oil, along with the onion, garlic and ginger. Fry them gently until they are soft and fragrant, but not brown, then remove them from the wok.

3   Heat 1 tbs oil in the wok and add one lightly beaten egg. Swirl the egg around to create a thin omelette and season it with salt and white pepper. When the egg has set, remove the omelette from the wok, roll it up and slice it very thinly. Repeat with more oil and the other egg. While you're waiting for the egg to set, cook the peas according to the directions on the packet.

4   Put the remaining oil in the wok over high heat. Add the rice and stir-fry it in the oil, then stir through the Chinese five-spice and soy sauce. When all the rice is well coated with soy and has a fairly dry consistency, add the egg, bacon, onion mixture and peas, and then toss to combine before removing the wok from the heat. Just before serving, stir through two-thirds of the shallots. Serve the rice topped with the remaining shallots and the crispy shallots.

*Note*: Crispy shallots can usually be found in the Asian section of the supermarket.

# Red lentil dhal

## serves 10

Preparation time: 5 minutes
Cooking time: about 25 minutes

This dhal recipe is a part of my friend Helene's New Year's Day feast, along with the yellow ghee rice overleaf, and the pork curry on page 47. These dishes are served alongside all the traditional Sri Lankan condiments and accompaniments, and the New Year is brought in with a bang!

2 cups (380 g) split red lentils
2 tbs oil or ghee
1 tsp black mustard seeds
1 large onion, finely sliced

6 dried curry leaves
1 tbs ground turmeric
270 ml can coconut milk

1  Place the lentils in a sieve and wash them under cold water until it runs clear. Remove any discoloured lentils. Place the lentils and 4 cups (1 litre) of water in a large saucepan. Cover and bring to the boil, then uncover and cook over low heat for about 15 minutes, until the lentils are very soft. Stir often to prevent them catching on the bottom and sticking.

2  Meanwhile, heat the oil or ghee in a frying pan and fry the mustard seeds on high heat until they start to pop. Add the onion, curry leaves and turmeric and continue frying for about 10 minutes over medium heat until the onion is very soft.

3  Add the onion mixture and coconut milk to the lentils, then stir to combine and heat through. The mixture should have a soft, runny consistency. Season with salt to taste and serve with savoury yellow ghee rice (see overleaf).

# Savoury yellow ghee rice

## serves 10

Preparation time: 5 minutes + 1 hour draining
Cooking time: 35 minutes

This rice is another of Helene's specialties. To bruise the cardamom pods, put them on a chopping board and give them a whack with the broad side of the blade of a large knife.

| | |
|---|---|
| 2 cups (450 g) basmati rice | 6 cardamom pods, bruised |
| 3 tbs ghee | 1 cinnamon stick, broken in half |
| 1 large onion, finely sliced | 3½ cups (825 ml) hot chicken stock |
| 1½ tsp ground turmeric | coriander leaves, to serve |
| 5–6 whole cloves | |

1  Place the rice in a sieve and wash it under the cold tap until the water runs clear, then spread it on a clean tea towel to drain for an hour.

2  Heat the ghee in a large saucepan and fry the onion over medium heat for about 10 minutes, until it is soft and golden. Add the rice and spices to the pan and continue frying until the rice is coated with ghee.

3  Pour the hot chicken stock in the pan, then cover it and bring it to the boil. Reduce the heat to very low and then cook, covered, for 20 minutes.

4  Remove the lid and cook for a further 5 minutes. Gently fluff up the rice grains with a fork and remove the whole spices before serving. Garnish with coriander.

*'Always be aware of the world around you and count your blessings.' – Marlene*

# Spring greens

## serves 4 as an accompaniment

Preparation time: 10 minutes
Cooking time: 10 minutes

Springtime vegetables are fresh and glorious. They don't need much help to taste sensational.

1 garlic clove
20 g butter, at room temperature
12 green beans, tailed

12 young asparagus spears, trimmed
12 snow peas, topped
salt and cracked black pepper, to taste

1 Preheat the oven to 180°C (160°C fan-forced). Roast the garlic clove whole, in its skin, for 10 minutes. When it has cooled slightly, squeeze the flesh out of the clove and mash it into the butter. (You won't want to turn the oven on to roast a single clove of garlic, so if you're not cooking something else at the same time, just sauté your garlic gently in butter until it's fragrant.)

2 Meanwhile, cook the vegetables. They can be steamed, blanched or microwaved if you prefer. To blanch them, bring a medium saucepan of water to the boil and have a bowl of cold water standing by. Put the beans into the boiling water for about 45 seconds, and the asparagus and snow peas for about 30 seconds – long enough to be 'tender-crisp' (I can't remember where I read this description but it fits here perfectly) – and then dunk them very quickly in the cold water.

3 Drain the greens and place them in a bowl, then toss through the garlic butter and season to taste.

*Note:* This side dish is pictured with the chicken parmigiana on page 36.

# Asian greens

## serves 4 as an accompaniment

Preparation time: 10 minutes
Cooking time: 5 minutes

I love this dish for its freshness and simplicity. It is not only the perfect accompaniment for Asian-style dishes, but also goes beautifully with simple grilled meat or fish.

| | |
|---|---|
| 4 baby bok choy | 1 tbs oyster sauce |
| 1 bunch (about 8 pieces) broccolini | 1 tbs sesame seeds, toasted |
| 2 tsp peanut oil | |

1   Discard any tough outer leaves of the bok choy. Wash the remaining leaves thoroughly, then trim the stems and cut them into quarters lengthways.

2   Cook the broccolini in a steamer for 2 minutes, then add the bok choy, steaming for a further 3 minutes. Alternatively, microwave them until they're tender but still slightly crisp.

3   Toss the greens with the peanut oil, then place them in a serving dish, drizzle them with oyster sauce and scatter sesame seeds on top.

*Note*: These greens are great with the marinated chicken wings on page 38.

# 4 | Special occasion dinners

I heard recently that dinner parties were making a comeback. I didn't know they'd gone anywhere! I love the theatre and the anticipation of a night out in a top-notch restaurant, I enjoy being waited on and trying new foods and flavour combinations, but for a great night with friends, I love to entertain at home – or go to their place. Because we have children, we often take turns with our friends to get together in our homes.

What is especially nice about hosting a dinner party is that you can create the atmosphere. You choose the music that's played, and the ambient lighting. You can play with the table setting – it can be as elaborate, or simply elegant, or quirky, or casual as you wish. I love the idea that at the end of the meal you can move to the comfy lounge. You can undo your belt a notch and kick your shoes off. You can talk and laugh until the small hours, if you want to.

I believe in the power of a good dinner party. I would love to see the next UN summit become a potluck dinner. Instead of interminable speeches, world leaders could lob up with a casserole, sit down around a table and break bread together. And with bellies full, amidst recipe swapping and laughter, the world's ills would be cured. It's a nice dream, anyway.

In this chapter, most recipes give servings for four, and are presented individually plated – but by all means, change that if you like. Quantities can be easily adjusted to suit a romantic dinner for two or a celebration for eight. For a casual dinner party, heaped platters of food in the centre of the table are great, promoting the feeling of community, friendship and sharing.

We normally save the term 'special occasion' for birthdays, anniversaries or important events, but I would suggest that every day is its own special occasion – that every time busy friends, harried parents or far-flung families can coordinate themselves to gather together, it is worthy of celebration. I declare this weekend a special occasion. Who's coming to dinner?

# Roast tomato soup

## serves 4

..............................................

Preparation time: 15 minutes
Cooking time: 55 minutes

Don't be put off by this recipe's long cooking time – most of it is just oven roasting.
This is a great dish for a dinner party as it can be made ahead of time and reheated.

2 kg ripe, red tomatoes
1 bulb garlic
¼ cup (60 ml) olive oil
salt and freshly ground pepper, to taste

2 cups (500 ml) chicken
or vegetable stock
2 tbs cream, to serve
crusty bread or croutons, to serve

1 Preheat the oven to 180°C (160°C fan-forced). Line a large baking tray with non-stick baking paper. Cut the tomatoes in half and arrange them on the baking tray, cut side up. Cut the top off the garlic bulb and place it on the tray too, cut side up. Drizzle with the olive oil and sprinkle with salt and pepper. Roast for about 45 minutes, until the tomatoes are soft and collapsing.

2 Cool the tomatoes until they are just warm, then place them in a food processor and squeeze in the roasted garlic. Process until smooth. Strain the liquid through a sieve into a saucepan, pressing with the back of a spoon to remove the skin and seed remnants (this takes a bit of work – you want to extract as much of the liquid as possible).

3 Add the stock and bring to the boil. Reduce the heat and simmer, uncovered, for 10–15 minutes or until the soup thickens to the consistency you like. Season to taste, then serve with a swirl of cream, a grind of black pepper and fresh crusty bread or croutons.

*'Use the good china. Every day is a special occasion.' – Nan*

*'Live it up! Life is too short not to.' – Marlene*

# Seafood chowder

## serves 6 as an entree, 4 as a main meal

Preparation time: 20 minutes
Cooking time: 50 minutes

This is Mum's recipe and has been a dinner party staple for as long as I can remember.
I have changed it a little bit: Mum uses oysters in hers; I prefer to leave them out and use
mussels instead. Taking recipes and adapting them to suit your own taste or the taste of your
family and friends is all a part of the cooking adventure. To vary this soup, try serving it with
crispy, very thin batons of bacon scattered on top, or with fried croutons for crunch.

1 cup (250 ml) white wine

12 mussels, shells scrubbed, beard removed

2 tbs olive oil

4 tbs (80 g) butter

200 g boneless, skinless white fish fillets,
cut into 6 pieces

200 g boneless, skinless salmon fillet,
cut into 6 pieces

12 green king prawns, peeled and deveined,
tails intact

12 Tasmanian scallops, roe removed

2 brown shallots, sliced

2 garlic cloves, sliced

300 ml cream

sea salt and white pepper

2 tbs lemon juice

2 tsp fresh dill leaf tips

lemon cheeks, to serve

**Bechamel sauce**

50 g butter

⅓ cup (50 g) plain flour

300 ml milk

1  Bring the white wine to the boil in a large saucepan and add the mussels. Cover and steam
for 2–3 minutes or until opened. Set the mussels aside and reserve the liquid.

2  In a chef's pan or large deep frying pan, heat 2 tsp of the olive oil and 1 tbs (20 g) of the butter over
medium-high heat. Sauté the white fish fillet pieces until the flesh looks white, rather than grey, on
the outside, but is still slightly underdone. Set them aside with the mussels and repeat the process
with the salmon, then the prawns, then the scallops. Each piece of seafood should be just slightly
undercooked, as it will cook further when it is reheated and the hot soup is added.

*Continued next page . . .*

## Seafood chowder, *continued...*

3 Lower the heat and, in the same pan the seafood has been cooked in, sauté the shallots and garlic until they are translucent and soft, but don't let them brown. Use the reserved wine from cooking the mussels to deglaze the pan, then turn the heat down to a very gentle simmer while you make the bechamel sauce.

4 To make the bechamel sauce, melt the butter in the pan that the mussels were cooked in and add the flour. Stir constantly over medium heat until the mixture starts to bubble and come together. Add a little of the milk and stir until combined. Keep adding the milk gradually until it is all incorporated, stirring constantly. Simmer for a few minutes to ensure that the flour is well cooked.

5 Strain the shallots and garlic, discard the solids and return the liquid to the pan. Stir in the cream and bring back up to a simmer. Add the bechamel sauce little by little, whisking well after each addition until it's all incorporated. Taste and season with salt and pepper.

6 Once the soup is simmering gently, turn the heat off and stir in the lemon juice and dill leaf tips. Reheat the seafood briefly in the pan, then divide evenly and artistically among shallow soup bowls and pour the steaming hot soup over the top. Serve immediately with lemon cheeks on the side.

*'I was one of seven children. Every Sunday afternoon one of us would be called upon to help shell the big bundles of peas, and string and slice the beans which were picked from the garden for the roast lunch. We would always try to avoid this chore.' – Tony*

*'When entertaining, do as much as possible beforehand so you can enjoy the company of your guests.' – Marlene*

# Twice-baked three cheese soufflé

## makes 6

Preparation time: 30 minutes
Cooking time: 45–50 minutes

The beauty of this entree is that it can be made ahead, then just finished off
in the oven a few minutes before serving. I am a big fan of dinner party dishes
that allow the cook to spend time with the guests.

| | |
|---|---|
| 2 tsp butter | 50 g Gruyère cheese, grated |
| 1 small onion, finely chopped | 50 g tasty cheddar cheese, grated |
| 1 tbs finely chopped thyme leaves | 3 egg yolks |
| 80 g butter, extra | salt and white pepper |
| ½ cup (75 g) plain flour | 4 eggwhites |
| 400 ml milk | 3 cups (750 ml) thickened cream, extra |
| 2 tbs thickened cream | 40 g grated parmesan |
| 50 g parmesan cheese, grated | ¼ cup finely chopped chives, to serve |

1   Preheat the oven to 180°C (160°C fan-forced). Grease six 150 ml dariole moulds or ramekins
with butter. Melt the butter in a frying pan and add the onion and thyme. Cook over medium-low
heat until the onion is soft and translucent, then set aside.

2   Melt the extra butter in a medium saucepan and add the flour. Cook, stirring, for 1 minute.
Add a small amount of milk and stir to incorporate. Continue to add the milk gradually, stirring
until smooth after each addition, and continue until all the milk has been incorporated. Add in the
onion mixture, the thickened cream and the cheeses and keep stirring until the cheese has melted.
Allow to cool for 10 minutes, then add the egg yolks and season to taste.

3   Beat the eggwhites in a clean bowl until soft peaks form. Fold a little bit of the eggwhite into the
pan with the cheese sauce and mix well, then gently fold in the remaining eggwhite, taking care not
to lose volume. Spoon into the prepared dariole moulds, being careful not to drip mixture down the
sides. Place the moulds in a baking dish and fill the dish with enough hot water to come halfway up
their sides.

*Continued next page . . .*

Special occasion dinners

Twice-baked three cheese soufflé, *continued...*

4   Bake for 20 minutes or until the soufflés are risen, firm and golden. Allow to cool a little and turn upside down into individual gratin dishes. These can be cooled – even refrigerated – until they are ready to serve.

5   When ready to serve, pour ½ cup (125 ml) cream over each soufflé and top with about 2 tbs parmesan cheese. Bake for 15–20 minutes, until they rise a little and the topping is golden brown. Scatter some chopped chives over each soufflé before serving.

*'We wait until everyone is at the table before eating.' – Elizabeth*

*'TV off – all to be seated before eating – say grace – candles on special occasions – youngest washes up.' – Gabrielle*

*'One of our rules is no singing at the table (we do find it hard to stick to this, though).' – Natasha*

# Scallops with cauliflower puree and bacon crumble

## serves 4

Preparation time: 20 minutes
Cooking time: 15 minutes

The combination of cauliflower, bacon and scallop is just gorgeous. This is a lovely dinner party dish. The puree and the crumble can be prepared ahead, leaving only the puree to be reheated, the crumble refreshed in the pan and the scallops to be sautéed at the last minute.

½ cauliflower (about 500 g, trimmed)
1 cup (250 ml) milk
250 g unsalted butter
salt, to taste
3 rashers bacon, cut into an extremely fine dice (about 2 mm)

½ cup (20 g) coarse fresh breadcrumbs
1 tbs butter
1 tbs olive oil
12 fat scallops, preferably on the half-shell, roe removed
lemon wedges, to serve

1  Finely chop or process the cauliflower, then place it in a medium saucepan with enough milk to cover it, and bring it to the boil. Boil rapidly for 8 minutes, until it disintegrates when rubbed between your fingers.

2  Place the cooked cauliflower in a food processor with the butter and process until smooth. Add salt to taste. If you want a perfect puree, push the mixture through a fine metal sieve to remove any remaining lumps, then set it aside.

3  Sauté the bacon in a frying pan. When the bacon is starting to cook and release its fat, add the breadcrumbs. Stir continually, until the breadcrumbs are golden and the bacon pieces are crunchy. Taste and season with salt if required – this will depend on how salty the bacon is – then drain on a paper towel.

4  Heat the butter and oil in a hot frying pan. When it is foaming, add the scallops and cook for 1–2 minutes, until they are golden brown and turning opaque. Turn and cook for a further 30 seconds to 1 minute. Dollop roughly 1½ tbs cauliflower puree into the half-shells (or onto your serving dishes, if you don't have the half-shells). Settle a scallop on top of the puree and finish with a generous sprinkle of the bacon crumble. Serve with lemon wedges.

# Stuffed chicken thighs with prosciutto

## serves 4

Preparation time: 30 minutes + 30 minutes chilling
Cooking time: about 20 minutes

Use this recipe to turn chicken thigh fillets into a dinner party dish – it can be prepared beforehand, looks beautiful, and tastes gorgeous with the salty prosciutto and sweet apricot sauce.

4 skinless chicken thigh fillets
2 garlic cloves, crushed
1 tbs thyme leaves
salt and pepper, to taste
12–16 slices prosciutto

1 tsp olive oil
1 quantity apricot sauce (see overleaf)
1 quantity rich potato puree (page 71), to serve
extra thyme leaves, to serve

1 Flatten the chicken thighs gently with a meat mallet or rolling pin to make them an even thickness and trim any excess fat. Place them smooth side down and spread with garlic and thyme, then season with salt and pepper. Roll the thigh inward from a long side, enclosing the herbs.

2 Lay two or three slices of prosciutto vertically on a piece of foil, overlapping them slightly. (Use good-quality foil.) At about the halfway mark, lay another piece of prosciutto horizontally across them. Place the thigh roll at the bottom of the prosciutto and roll as tightly as you can toward the top. When you reach the horizontal piece of prosciutto, fold it over the ends of the roll and continue rolling until complete.

3 Place the roll at the edge of the foil and roll it up as tightly as you can. The foil should go around the thigh at least 5 or 6 times. Twist either end of the foil tightly, so it looks like a bonbon, and fold the ends over. Roll the package on the benchtop to achieve a uniform sausage shape.

4 Half fill a large pan with water and heat until simmering gently. Place the foil packages in the water and place a tea towel on top to keep them submerged. Return to a simmer and cook for 10 minutes, then remove the packages from the pan and place them in the fridge for half an hour. This helps them to maintain their shape.

5 Heat the olive oil in a frying pan over medium heat. Remove the foil from the chicken thighs and cook them in the oil, turning frequently, until golden brown on all sides. Cut into slices and serve drizzled with apricot sauce on a bed of rich potato puree. Sprinkle with extra thyme leaves.

# Apricot sauce

## serves 4

Preparation time: 5 minutes
Cooking time: 25 minutes

½ tsp olive oil

1 brown shallot, sliced

1 cup (250 ml) apricot nectar

1 cup (250 ml) chicken stock

1 tbs brown sugar

2 tbs white wine vinegar

1   Heat the olive oil in a saucepan and cook the shallot over medium heat until soft but not brown, then add all the other ingredients and simmer for 10 minutes.

2   Strain the sauce through a metal sieve and return it to the pan, then simmer for a further 10 minutes or until the sauce has reduced to a slightly syrupy consistency.

'One night when I was a kid, Aunty Joyce and Uncle Bob were coming over for a special dinner. Dad went to buy some drinks. The man at the hotel talked him into trying a new drink for ladies, which had just come on the market – Pimm's No. 1 Cup. Dad didn't read the instructions properly, so rather than serving it with ginger ale, he just poured it straight into long glasses and put a cherry, a mint leaf and a cucumber slice on top. Mum and Aunty Joyce just laughed and laughed and we couldn't get a bit of sense out of them. Dinner was served up at half past ten, completely ruined, and they didn't care a bit.' – Marlene

# Roast crown of chicken

## serves 4

Preparation time: 20 minutes + 30 minutes chilling
Cooking time: 40 minutes

You can ask your butcher to prepare a chicken 'on the crown' for you,
or you could buy a whole chicken and do it yourself. Here's how it is done:

First, remove the middle section and tips of the wings (reserve them for making gravy later).
Scrape clean the remaining wing bone (the one closest to the breast). To remove the leg
and thigh, cut through the skin and meat between the thigh and the body, then feel for the joint
and cut through to remove it fully. Keep as much skin as possible on the breast. Finally, take
a pair of kitchen scissors or a knife and remove the back of the chicken by cutting up
either side of the breast. You should be left with the double breast still attached to
the rib cage, with the bare wing bones sticking out.

200 g unsalted butter, at room temperature
finely grated zest of 1 lemon
¼ cup finely chopped fresh sage leaves
¼ cup finely chopped thyme leaves

2 crown roast of chicken (double breast on the bone)
salt and white pepper, to taste
1 tbs olive oil
1 quantity leek puree (see overleaf)

1   Preheat the oven to 200°C (180°C fan-forced). Mix the butter, lemon zest and herbs until they
    are well combined. Carefully separate the skin of the chicken breasts from the flesh and use
    your fingers to spread the butter between the flesh and skin. Tuck the skin neatly around the
    edges of the crown roast and season all over with salt and white pepper, then refrigerate for
    30 minutes, until the butter is firm.

2   Heat the oil in a heavy-based ovenproof pan over medium-high heat and sear the roasts, skin
    side down, for about 5 minutes, until golden brown. Turn the roasts skin side up and place them
    in the oven for 30 minutes, or until the meat is tender. Baste the skin with the pan juices from
    time to time.

3   Remove from the oven and set aside to rest for 10 minutes. Cut each crown in half to make
    four portions. Serve on a bed of leek puree and drizzle with reheated pan juices.

# Leek puree

## serves 4 as an accompaniment

Preparation time: 5 minutes
Cooking time: 5 minutes

The secret to a beautiful vegetable puree is to be true to the ingredient you are using.
Cook it as quickly as possible and don't drown it with other flavours.
This ensures that it bursts with fresh flavour.

3 leeks, trimmed of dark green,
finely sliced (about 2½ cups)

30 g unsalted butter
salt and white pepper, to taste

1   Slice the leeks very finely, or process in a food processor.

2   Place them in a large heavy-based pan and pour over just enough boiling water to cover them.
    Cover and return to the boil, then uncover and cook rapidly until very soft – around 3–4 minutes.

3   Drain the leeks and place them in a food processor with the butter. Process to a smooth puree.

4   Season to taste with salt and white pepper. Just before serving, reheat in a saucepan.

*'Whoever's birthday it is gets to choose what's for dinner.' – Daniel*

*'Every few months when we were kids, my brothers and sisters and I would block off
the kitchen with a sheet and cook a big three-course dinner. It was a lot of fun and we
made a massive mess. I am sure the food was average at best but Mum and Dad
made a big deal out of it.' – Mick*

*'Don't spoil a happy occasion with an argument.' – Nan*

# Roasted lamb rump with garlic and rosemary

## serves 4–6

Preparation time: 25 minutes
Cooking time: about 15 minutes + 10 minutes resting

It's no secret that I love lamb. This cut in particular is a favourite of mine,
as it gives you the rich, tender meat of a full roast leg, without the hours of cooking.

3 lamb rumps, around 350–400 g each,
trimmed of excess fat
2 garlic cloves, chopped
½ cup finely chopped fresh rosemary leaves
½ tsp garlic powder
salt and freshly ground black pepper, to taste
2 tbs olive oil

**Sauce**
½ cup (125 ml) white wine
1 garlic clove, extra, halved
1 rosemary sprig
½ cup (125 ml) good-quality liquid chicken stock

1   Preheat the oven to 180°C (160°C fan-forced). Turn each lamb rump upside down on your chopping board and carefully create a split lengthways, only cutting about two-thirds of the way through the meat. Combine the garlic and rosemary and then stuff the mixture into the incision in each rump. Tie them up with cooking twine to create a neat cylindrical shape.

2   Combine the garlic powder with plenty of salt and pepper and scatter it over a tray, then roll the lamb rumps in the seasoning until they are thoroughly coated.

3   Heat the olive oil in a heavy-based frying pan and sear the rumps until all sides are golden brown. Transfer to a baking tray or a frying pan with an ovenproof handle and bake for about 10 minutes. Test by piercing with a skewer: bright red indicates a little further cooking time is required; pink juices indicate a medium roast. Rest the meat for 10 minutes before serving.

4   Meanwhile, to make the sauce, deglaze the pan with the white wine. Add the garlic, rosemary and chicken stock. Bring to the boil and cook for 3–4 minutes, until reduced to about ⅔ of a cup. Slice the meat and serve drizzled with the sauce.

*'Make sure there is plenty of food and drink. If the food is great,*
*everyone will remember the occasion.' – Marcus*

# Salmon fillet with rich lemon sauce

## serves 2

Preparation time: 5 minutes
Cooking time: about 8 minutes

This is just one of a thousand things to do with beautiful fresh salmon fillets.
Serve them with zucchini ribbons and chat potatoes, or on a bed of homemade
linguine with a salad of green leaves.

1 tsp olive oil

2 × 180 g fresh salmon fillets, skin on

salt and freshly ground black pepper

½ cup (125 ml) thickened cream

1 tbs finely grated lemon zest

2 tsp butter

1 tbs lemon juice

1 egg yolk

2 tbs chopped dill

1 Heat a large non-stick frying pan over medium-high heat and add the olive oil. Place the salmon in the pan, skin side down. Season the top with a little salt and freshly ground black pepper. Using a spatula or an egg flip, press the fish gently so the skin has even contact with the surface – if left alone, it will curl up.

2 After about 3 minutes, turn the fish over and cook for a further 2 minutes. Remove it from the pan and let it rest, covered, in a warm place.

3 Meanwhile, in a separate pan, heat the cream and lemon zest over low heat until warm. Add the butter and lemon juice and stir to combine, then add the egg yolk and whisk until the sauce thickens. Just before serving, stir through the dill.

4 Serve the salmon drizzled with the sauce and whatever accompaniments you choose.

*'Entertain often – a houseful of friends is joyous.'* – Marlene

*'When pouring sherry, only pour half a glass. The top half.'* – Nan

Special occasion dinners

# Slow-roasted pork belly
# with cider-braised cabbage

## serves 4

.............................................................................

Preparation time: 30 minutes
Cooking time: 2 hours + 20 minutes resting

You may need to ask your butcher for this cut. Pork belly is most commonly sold
as 'pork rashers', which are narrow strips of belly, and usually have the bone in. This recipe
requires a whole piece of belly with the bones removed. Make sure the pork skin is very dry before
scoring and cooking it. It is best to leave it uncovered in the fridge for 24 hours before cooking.

1 kg piece of boneless pork belly
2 tsp olive oil
2 tsp salt
1 tbs olive oil, extra
¼ green cabbage, finely shredded
1 cup (250 ml) apple cider

salt and pepper, to taste
25 g butter
3 Granny Smith apples, peeled, cored
  and cut into thin wedges
1 tbs sugar

1  Preheat the oven to 220°C (200°C fan-forced). Using a Stanley knife or a Mickey knife, score
   the rind, cutting into the fat but not into the flesh. I like to score the rind in lines about 1 cm apart.
   Make sure the belly has no stray bristles on it, then rub the rind with the olive oil and massage
   the salt thoroughly into it.

2  Place the pork on a rack in a roasting pan, skin side up, and roast for 30 minutes or until the
   skin begins to puff up and look crisp. Pour some water into the base of the roasting pan from
   time to time so the juices won't burn.

3  Turn the oven down to 160°C (140°C fan-forced) and continue to roast the pork, uncovered,
   for a further 1½ hours. Remove from the oven and let rest for about 20 minutes.

4  Meanwhile, heat the extra olive oil in a chef's pan or large deep frying pan over medium-high heat.
   Add the cabbage and cook, stirring occasionally, for about 5 minutes, until it begins to soften and
   collapse. Add the cider, bring to a simmer and cook for about 10 minutes, until it reduces. Season
   with salt and pepper.

5  Heat the butter in a frying pan until it's foaming, then add the apples and stir until they begin
   to soften. Add the sugar and cook over medium-low heat for about 10 minutes, stirring occasionally,
   until the apples have fully softened and caramelised. Serve the pork belly in thick slices on a bed of
   cabbage, accompanied by the apples.

# 5 | Desserts

When my mother was growing up, dessert was an essential part of the evening meal. Whether it was a cooked pudding, or bread and bananas, there was always something sweet to finish things off.

Nan made lots of baked rice puddings, which only had rice, sugar and milk. These were put in a dish and baked slowly until the rice absorbed the milk. A golden film would form on top, and the pudding would be thick and creamy and sweet on the inside. Well, that was the plan, anyway. Because Nan didn't follow recipes (or maybe because she forget the puddings were in the oven), she never made two the same. Sometimes it would be well and truly overcooked and dry; other times it would have too much milk and be watery; and then there were times it was just right. When Mum complained, Nan would say being predictable was boring.

It would seem, in fact, that Nan had her share of cooking disasters, and not only with the rice pudding. Her family never cottoned on until my grandfather decided to get rid of a huge sprawling bush that was taking over a corner of the yard. As he got rid of the bush, so the story goes, he discovered over a dozen burnt pots and pans hidden under it. He asked Nan about it and she confessed that sometimes she would get talking on the phone and would burn the dinner beyond salvation. Her solution to the problem was to throw the pot in the bush.

My own memories of Nan's cooking were not of disasters. I remember big plates of corned beef with white sauce, and beef stroganoff, and beautiful baked dinners. I remember the smell of Nan's place, the scratchy woollen blankets when we slept over, and the many singalongs around the pianola. I remember the rock cakes in a tin and real tea made in a teapot. I remember warm banana custard, and pikelets with butter and jam, and apple crumble with ice-cream. I remember that, just like when Mum was a kid, when we ate tea at Nan's we got big helpings, it was piping hot, and there was always dessert to finish. And we knew beyond a shadow of a doubt that we were loved.

# Lemon meringue pudding

## serves 6–8

Preparation time: 15 minutes + cooling and chilling
Cooking time: 10–12 minutes

With eleven children to feed and a home-based business to support them, it's no surprise that a number of Mick's grandmother's recipes had one eye on economy. This recipe uses no milk or cream, and hardly any butter – a couple of eggs, a couple of lemons, a handful of sugar. It costs very little to put on the table, and yet it is absolutely delicious and decadent.

⅓ cup (45 g) cornflour
600 ml water
1 cup (220 g) caster sugar
juice and finely grated zest of 2 lemons

2 eggs, separated
30 g unsalted butter
2 tbs caster sugar, extra

1   Put the cornflour into a saucepan (off the heat), and stir in a little of the water to form a smooth paste. Add the rest of the water and stir over medium heat until the mixture boils and thickens, stirring constantly to avoid lumps forming.

2   Remove from the heat and add the sugar, lemon juice and zest, and the 2 egg yolks. Return to the stove and stir for about 5 minutes, until thickened. Stir in the butter. Pour into a 24 cm pie dish. Cool slightly, then refrigerate for 30 minutes, until set.

3   Preheat the oven to 200°C (180°C fan-forced). Beat the eggwhites until soft peaks form. Add the extra sugar and beat until stiff peaks form. Pile the meringue onto the lemon pudding and spread to cover the surface. Bake for 10–12 minutes, until it starts to look golden brown. Serve cold.

*'God will provide.' – Grandma*

*'Waste not, want not.' – Nan*

# Appelbeignets

## makes about 48

.....................................................................................................

Preparation time: 20 minutes
Cooking time: 3 minutes per batch

This recipe comes from my friend Megan. Her dad, Burt, grew up in a small town in the Netherlands and emigrated to Australia with his parents after World War II. Megan's mum, Mary, is an Aussie girl, but she took her husband's Dutch heritage to heart and made a loving effort to learn recipes from his childhood. This is one of them. Appelbeignets are delicious hot. They are also delicious when the leftovers are surreptitiously sneaked from the fridge. Warning: you have to make a lot for there to be any leftovers.

| | |
|---|---|
| 6 apples, peeled and cored | 375 ml beer |
| 1⅔ cups (250 g) plain flour | oil for deep-frying |
| pinch of salt | icing sugar mixture, to dust |

1   Cut the apples crossways into 5 mm slices. Sift the flour and salt into a large bowl and make a well in the centre. Gradually add the beer, stirring constantly until the mixture is smooth.

2   Half fill a large saucepan with oil and heat it to about 190°C.

3   Working a few at a time, dip the apple slices into the batter and cook them in the hot oil for about 3 minutes, until they are crisp and golden. Transfer to a large tray lined with paper towels to drain. Cool slightly, then sprinkle generously with icing sugar and serve.

*'I loved it when we would go for a drive to the country and buy fruit by the case. We would spend an afternoon peeling and coring Granny Smith apples. Mum would then stew them and freeze them and we would have them with ice-cream or custard for dessert. When I was old enough, she let me help make the custard.' – Paul*

*'My mum handmade everything when I was a kid. I would sit with her in the kitchen and watch her peel these huge green cooking apples – not with a peeler but with a knife. It was very impressive to me. My brother and I would eat the peels and Mum would make beautiful apple pie and crumble.' – Steph*

# Cream horns

## makes 32

........................................................................................................

Preparation time: 20 minutes
Cooking time: 10 minutes per batch

I can't remember a big family gathering that didn't have trays full of this favourite.
Christenings, engagements, birthday parties . . . if there was going to be a gathering,
Mum would get baking on the cream horns. They're a great finger-food dessert and
loved by all. Cream horn moulds are available from kitchenware shops.

4 sheets frozen puff pastry     1 quantity mock cream (see overleaf)

1 egg     icing sugar, to dust

⅔ cup (220 g) strawberry jam

1    Preheat the oven to 200°C (180°C fan-forced). Lightly grease two large baking trays and line
with non-stick baking paper. Remove the pastry sheets from the freezer for a few minutes
to thaw before beginning, but don't allow them to become too soft, as they will be difficult
to handle. Cut each pastry sheet into eight strips.

2    Take a cream horn mould, holding the open end in your left hand if you are right-handed, or vice
versa. Pick up a strip of pastry with your right hand and press it gently onto the pointed end of the
horn tin, with the pastry strip hanging down on the side closest to you. Carefully turn the tin away
from you as you guide the pastry around it, overlapping the pastry by about 5–7 mm, until you come
to the end of the strip. Don't take the pastry too close to the open end of the horn mould, as it will
puff over the edge while cooking, making it difficult to remove.

3    Place the pastry-covered moulds on the baking trays, leaving plenty of space between them.
Make sure the end of the pastry is underneath, so the horn will hold its shape. Lightly beat the
egg with 1 tbs of water and brush it over the pastry to glaze. Bake for 10–15 minutes, or until rich
golden brown. Remove from the oven and allow to cool for few minutes, then carefully slide the
cases off the moulds. Cool the horns on a wire rack. Repeat with remaining pastry.

4    Using a piping bag with a plain 3 mm nozzle, pipe strawberry jam into the bottom of each horn
and a stripe up the inside. Next, using a clean piping bag with a plain 1 cm nozzle, fill the horns
with the mock cream. Arrange the horns on a serving platter and lightly sift icing sugar over
them to decorate.

*'Favourite dessert – Mum's cream horns! Go, Mum.' – Debbie*

# Mock cream

## makes 1 cup

Preparation time: 10 minutes
No cooking time

This is my mum's mock cream, used to fill the cream horns on the previous page.
It can also be used between layers of a cake, or in neenish or pineapple tarts.

250 g unsalted butter, cubed        2 tsp powdered gelatine
⅓ cup (75 g) caster sugar        ½ tsp cream of tartar
1 tsp vanilla essence

1   Combine the butter and sugar in an electric mixer. Beat on slow speed until combined, then
    increase speed to high and beat until light and creamy. Add the vanilla essence and continue
    to beat on high until the sugar has dissolved.

2   Place ½ cup cold water in a small bowl. Sprinkle the gelatine over and let it soften, then stand the
    bowl in a pan of hot water and whisk with a fork until the gelatine is thoroughly dissolved. Cool
    to room temperature. Add one teaspoonful of this mixture to the butter mixture at a time, beating
    constantly. Sprinkle the cream of tartar evenly into the butter mixture and continue to beat until it
    is creamy, light in colour and smooth in consistency.

*'About once a month we got Neapolitan ice-cream.
We had to have equal amounts of each flavour.' – Mick*

*'We had ice-cream with different toppings for dessert – strawberry,
chocolate, lime topping, Milo, or tinned fruit.' – Rebecca*

# Ginger syrup sponge

## makes 4

Preparation time: 30 minutes
Cooking time: about 30 minutes

These light little syrupy sponges are an alternative to sticky date pudding –
not as dense or creamy, but with a fresh lovely ginger flavour.

1 quantity almond praline (see overleaf)
1 tbs soft unsalted butter
½ cup (100 g) brown sugar
1 egg
½ cup (125 ml) milk
1 tbs golden syrup

1 cup (150 g) self-raising flour
2 tsp ground ginger
2 tsp ground cinnamon
½ cup (110 g) caster sugar
5 cm piece of fresh ginger, peeled and sliced thinly
vanilla ice-cream, to serve

1  Preheat the oven to 160°C (140°C fan-forced). Make your praline first, using the recipe on the following page, and set it aside to cool. Grease four 200 ml capacity dariole moulds. Using electric beaters, beat the butter and brown sugar until light and creamy. Whisk the egg, milk and golden syrup in a jug. Add gradually to the butter mixture, beating constantly.

2  Sift together the flour, ginger and cinnamon. Gently fold into the wet ingredients, then pour into the prepared moulds (they will only be half full, but the sponges will rise up when cooked). Bake for 20 minutes or until springy when touched on top. Remove from the oven and turn out of the dariole moulds. Wash and dry the moulds.

3  Meanwhile, put the caster sugar in a small saucepan with ½ cup (125 ml) water and stir over low heat until the sugar dissolves. Add the fresh ginger and bring to the boil. Cook until reduced to about two-thirds of the original volume, or until it has reached a syrupy consistency.

4  Return the sponges to the moulds and pierce them several times with a skewer. Pour a tablespoonful of syrup over each sponge. Continue to 'feed' the sponges in this way, allowing the syrup to soak in, until all but 3 tablespoonfuls of the syrup (¼ cup or 60 ml) has been used.

5  To serve, break the almond praline into shards. Cut a small slice off the top of each sponge to make it level. Place upside down on serving plates and drizzle with the remaining syrup. Top with shards of almond praline and serve with a scoop of vanilla ice-cream.

# Almond praline

## makes about 350 g

Preparation time: 5 minutes
Cooking time: about 12 minutes

Praline can be made using toasted sesame seeds, roast peanuts
or macadamias, or your favourite chopped nuts.

½ cup (65 g) slivered almonds, toasted    1 cup (220 g) caster sugar

1   Place a sheet of non-stick baking paper on a baking tray and evenly distribute the toasted almonds over it, roughly covering a 22 cm round area.

2   Combine 1 cup (220 g) of the sugar and 1 cup (250 ml) water in a small saucepan and stir over low heat, without boiling, to dissolve the sugar. Increase the heat to high and bring to the boil. Cook for about 10–12 minutes, until it starts to turn a pale golden brown. This is the point where you will need to watch it very carefully, as it darkens quite quickly. The trick is knowing when to remove the caramel from the heat. If you do it while it's still too pale, it won't develop the lovely deep toffee flavour you want, but if it's too dark it will taste burnt. The best description I can give is that it needs to be about the colour of golden syrup. It will continue to cook as you take it off the heat, so moments before it's the right colour, take it off the stove.

3   Let the bubbles subside, then drizzle the toffee evenly over the almonds to cover them completely. The toffee should be about 2–3 mm thick. Set aside to cool and harden.

*'When I was a little kid the first thing I learned to cook was chocolate pudding.
I made it so often I knew the recipe off by heart. Maybe that's why I was a little
tubby as a kid. It gave me a buzz when I made it for visitors and was
complimented on how good it tasted.' – Josh*

# Milk chocolate pots

## makes 6

....................................................................................................

Preparation time: 30 minutes
Cooking time: 1 hour + chilling

Many chocolate desserts use dark chocolate for its richness and delicious bitterness.
These desserts are made with milk chocolate – it's lighter, almost a return to the smooth,
cold chocolate custard of childhood. This dessert needs to be planned in advance because of the
time it takes to chill. The beauty of it is, the little pots emerge from the fridge ready to serve –
with some ripe raspberries and cream, some almond biscuits, or just on their own.

**Custard**

½ cup (110 g) caster sugar
1½ cups (375 ml) milk
1½ cups (375 ml) thickened cream
1 vanilla pod, cut in half, or 1 tsp vanilla extract
250 g milk cooking chocolate, chopped
6 egg yolks

**Ganache**

125 g milk cooking chocolate, grated
or processed finely
1 cup (250 ml) thickened cream

1   To make the custard, preheat the oven to 120°C (100°C fan-forced). Combine the sugar, milk,
    cream and vanilla in a medium saucepan and stir over medium heat until scalding but not quite
    boiling. Add the chocolate and stir until melted.

2   Whisk the egg yolks in a bowl until pale and frothy. Slowly add the hot milk mixture, stirring
    vigorously. Whisk until all the ingredients are well combined.

3   Pour the mixture into six 150 ml ramekins or ovenproof glasses. Place the ramekins in a baking
    dish and fill it with enough hot water to come halfway up their sides, then bake for an hour. When
    done they will still seem to be slightly liquid, but they will set further in the fridge. Refrigerate for
    several hours until firm.

4   Meanwhile, to make the ganache, place the chocolate in a bowl. Bring the cream to boiling point
    and pour it over the chocolate, stirring with a metal spoon or silicone spatula. Set aside at room
    temperature while the custards bake and cool.

5   When the custards have set in the fridge, pour the ganache over them in a layer about 2–3 mm
    thick. Return them to the fridge for another hour or so until the ganache has set. Serve just as
    they are, or top with a few berries.

# Orange syrup cake with white chocolate and yoghurt ganache

## serves 10–12

Preparation time: 30 minutes
Cooking time: about 50–60 minutes

This is a great winter dessert, especially on the Central Coast of New South Wales where I live. The area was once covered by vast citrus orchards and there are still orange and lemon trees in many backyards. Winter to me means being given bags of oranges by friends and neighbours, and cooking all sorts of lovely things with them.

250 g unsalted butter
200 g caster sugar
finely grated zest of 2 oranges
4 eggs
1⅔ cups (250 g) self-raising flour
1 tsp ground ginger
2 oranges, segmented (see note, page 54)

**Syrup**
1 cup (220 g) caster sugar
1 cup (250 ml) orange juice

**Ganache**
125 g white chocolate
½ cup (140 g) plain yoghurt

1   Preheat the oven to 150°C (130°C fan-forced). Grease a 26 cm round springform tin and line it with baking paper. Using electric beaters, beat the butter and sugar until light and creamy. Beat in the orange zest, then add the eggs one at a time, beating to incorporate each one.

2   Sift the flour and ginger together, then fold gently through the butter mixture. Pour into the prepared cake tin and smooth the top. Bake for 50–60 minutes, or until golden brown and springy when touched on top.

3   Meanwhile, to make the syrup, place the caster sugar and orange juice in a small saucepan. Stir over low heat to dissolve the sugar, then increase the heat to high and bring to the boil, skimming off any scum that comes to the surface. Reduce the heat slightly and simmer for about 10 minutes, until it is reduced to 1¼ cups (310 ml).

*Continued next page …*

Orange syrup cake with white chocolate and yoghurt ganache, *continued...*

4   Remove the cake from the oven and pierce the top all over with a skewer. Feed spoonfuls of the syrup over it. Continue this until most of the syrup has been used, reserving a few spoonfuls for serving. Leave to cool completely.

5   To make the ganache, melt the chocolate in a bowl over a pan of simmering water. Once melted, allow to cool slightly. Stir in the yoghurt and chill until serving time.

6   Remove the cake from the tin and peel away the baking paper. Serve wedges of the cake with a dollop of white chocolate ganache and orange segments, drizzled in the reserved syrup.

*'Make sure there's not a speck of yolk in the eggwhites or they won't beat properly.'* – Grandma

*'When Mum used to cook cakes we would all fight over the spoon, the spatula and the beaters. The best part was the bowl – we all fought over that and had to take turns.'* – Rebecca

*'To whip cream make sure it's cold and the beaters and bowl are completely dry.'* – Nan

120

Puddings

# Crème brûlée

## makes 6

Preparation time: 20 minutes
Cooking time: 5 minutes + 6 hours chilling

I met some people at a party recently who are mad crème brûlée fans. They have
an interesting policy: when eating out, if the menu of the restaurant has crème brûlée on it,
they are compelled to order it. Apparently the rule dictates that no matter how full they are
after the meal, they have to see the dessert menu, in case they need to order the brûlée.
I personally consider this an admirable policy and one which should be adopted by more people.
Dessert does go into a separate stomach, after all. There is always room for crème brûlée.

| | |
|---|---|
| 600 ml thickened cream | 8 egg yolks |
| 1 tsp vanilla extract | ⅓ cup (75 g) caster sugar |
| 1 tsp finely grated lemon zest | ¼ cup (55 g) caster sugar, extra, to top |

1   Place the cream, vanilla and lemon zest into a medium saucepan over medium-high heat and
    bring almost to the boil. Meanwhile, whisk the egg yolks and sugar until thick and pale.

2   Strain the cream into the eggs, stirring constantly. Wash and dry the saucepan and return the
    mixture to it. Stir continuously over low heat for about 5 minutes, until the custard thickens.
    To test for the correct thickness, dip a wooden spoon into the custard. Run your finger along the
    back of the spoon. If the trail left by your finger stays intact, the custard is thick enough. If it runs,
    or if the custard 'bleeds' into the mark left by your finger, it needs longer. When it is ready, pour it
    into six 150 ml ramekins. Refrigerate for at least 6 hours, until set and well chilled.

3   Just before serving, sprinkle caster sugar over the whole surface of the custard, making sure
    there are no gaps. Depending on the surface area of your ramekin, you will need about 1½–2 tsp
    per brûlée. Using a kitchen blowtorch, heat the sugar until it bubbles and turns golden brown.
    If you like a nice thick caramel topping (as I do), repeat this process. Leave the toffee for a few
    minutes to cool and set before serving.

Note: Have a sinkful of cold water ready in case the custard begins to split. You will know this is
happening if the texture becomes grainy instead of silky smooth. If this happens, put the saucepan
straight into the sink, add ¼ cup (60 ml) cold cream and whisk like the clappers. With any luck,
the custard will come back together. Return it to the heat if it's not thick enough (be vigilant!).

# Passionfruit puddle pie

## serves 12

Preparation time: 1 hour + lots of chilling
Cooking time: about 40 minutes

After the rather public collapse of my passionfruit custard flan not too long ago,
I have revisited the recipe to make it work. The secret ingredient is time –
time to let the pastry cool before it is turned out of the flan tin, and time
to let the crème pâtissière cool down and set in the flan.

The recipe makes one large flan to cut and serve, but it can also be used to make
twelve little flans that pack a big passionfruit flavour. Big or small, I am happy
to report that they will not look like a puddle.

**White chocolate ganache**
125 g white chocolate, chopped
½ cup (125 ml) thickened cream

**Pastry**
1¾ cups (265 g) plain flour
¼ cup (35 g) icing sugar mixture
125 g cold unsalted butter, cubed
1 egg, lightly beaten

**Passionfruit syrup**
pulp of 4 passionfruit
¼ cup (55 g) caster sugar

**Passionfruit crème pâtissière**
pulp of 8 passionfruit
400 ml thickened cream
1 vanilla bean, split, or 1 tsp vanilla extract
1 wide strip lemon zest (peeled with a knife
   from a lemon)
4 egg yolks
125 g caster sugar
⅓ cup (50 g) cornflour
50 g butter, cubed

Passionfruit puddle pie, *continued...*

1   To make the white chocolate ganache, place the chocolate and cream in a heat-proof bowl over a pan of simmering water. Make sure the bowl is not touching the water. As the chocolate starts to soften, stir until it melts and combines with the cream. Transfer to a different bowl (as the first one will be hot) and refrigerate for 2½ hours, stirring occasionally, until thickened.

2   To make the pastry, place the flour and icing sugar into a food processor and add the butter. Process in short bursts until the mixture has a fine crumb consistency. Add the egg and process again in short bursts until the mixture just starts to come together.

3   Turn out onto a work surface and gather the dough together. Press out to a thick disc, wrap in cling wrap and refrigerate for 15 minutes.

4   When it has chilled, roll out the dough on a sheet of non-stick baking paper to fit a 26 cm loose-based flan tin. Line the tin with the pastry, easing it into the corners. If the pastry breaks at all, just patch it together gently, then trim the overhanging pastry and refrigerate for 30 minutes. Meanwhile, preheat the oven to 180°C (160°C fan-forced).

5   Cover the pastry with a sheet of non-stick baking paper and fill it with rice or pastry weights. Blind bake the pastry for 15 minutes, remove the weights and paper and bake it again for a further 10–15 minutes or until light golden brown. Remove from the oven and cool completely.

6   To make the passionfruit syrup, place the passionfruit pulp and sugar in a small saucepan with ½ cup (125 ml) water. Stir over low heat to dissolve the sugar, then bring to the boil, skimming the froth off the top as you go. Boil for about 2 minutes, until syrupy, then remove from the heat and cool.

7   To make the passionfruit crème pâtissière, place the passionfruit pulp into a strainer over a bowl and leave it to strain. Scald the cream by heating it in a saucepan with the vanilla bean and lemon zest until it is just about to boil. Whisk the egg yolks and sugar in a bowl until light and creamy. Strain the cream and pour over the egg yolks, whisking all the time.

Passionfruit puddle pie, *continued...*

8   Wash and dry the saucepan and then pour the mixture back in. Add the cornflour and whisk
    to combine. Stir over very low heat for about 5 minutes. As the mixture starts to thicken,
    whisk a bit more quickly until it is thick and smooth. Pour onto a tray and cover the surface with
    cling wrap. Refrigerate for 10 minutes, until the mixture is just warmer than room temperature.

9   Remove the mixture from the fridge and transfer it to a bowl, then beat in the butter and the juice
    from the strained passionfruit pulp. Fill the pastry case with this mixture and then spread the
    white chocolate ganache over the top. Drizzle with the passionfruit syrup and refrigerate for about
    4 hours. When the filling has chilled and set, cut the pie into wedges and serve with a dollop of
    double cream or a scoop of vanilla ice-cream.

Desserts

# 6 | Sweet treats

I first met Imelda Henebery when I started going out with her grandson, now my husband Mick. I clearly recall the array of baked goods that were whipped out of Tupperware and ice-cream containers and spread on the table every time we went to visit her and Grandpa. I became familiar with the sight of her famous decorated sponge cakes at all the family events. I had never seen sponge cakes so huge – some over a metre long and half as wide – or tasted any so light and delicious.

Of course, Grandma had to make huge cakes. She had eleven children, and at the time of her passing in 2002 at age eighty she had thirty-three grandchildren and twelve great-grandchildren. That number now stands at thirty-four grandchildren and twenty-eight great-grandchildren. Family was one of the great joys of Grandma's life, and she embodied the philosophy that cooking is a powerful and nurturing way to show love.

When I asked her family to talk to me about Grandma and her cooking, there was a tremendous outpouring of memories. The theme that occurred over and over again was abundance – the generosity, the variety, and the joy with which Grandma provided everything. 'I used to love that I never seemed to be told that only one was allowed,' says Imelda's granddaughter Rebecca. 'I don't have one memory of being told that I could not have more.' Another granddaughter, Sarah, agrees. 'What I remember was the abundance and the variety to choose from. If the word please was used we were never denied.'

Imelda Henebery's legacy lives in the lessons that she passed on to her children, who have passed it on to theirs, who are in turn teaching their own. It lives in the memories that she created, and in the huge family celebrations that continue today. It lives in her descendants and the special closeness they share – a closeness that is not always easy or common among very large families. And it lives in her recipes, written in copperplate and cooked with love – first by her, and now by those who have come after her. Cooking from her recipes and talking about her is a tangible way of bringing Grandma back – through her food and the memories it evokes.

# Grandma's hazelnut chocolate biscuits

## makes about 45

Preparation time: 20 minutes
Cooking time: about 12 minutes per batch

Carmel, Grandma's daughter, remembers travelling to Queensland when she was just eighteen, full of a sense of adventure at moving far away from home. While unpacking the box of essential household items that her mother had sent with her, she came across two enormous tins filled to the brim with her favourite biscuits – these hazelnut cookies.

'A wave of homesickness washed over my head,' says Carmel. 'Not because I would miss my favourite foods (which I would), but because of what those tins represented – home, warmth, and the person who knew what my favourite bikkies were, my mum.'

| | |
|---|---|
| 185 g unsalted butter | good pinch of salt |
| 1 cup (220 g) caster sugar | 60 g ground or finely chopped hazelnuts |
| 1 egg | (or almonds) |
| ½ tsp vanilla essence | 60 g chopped dark chocolate, or choc bits |
| 2 cups (300 g) self-raising flour | ½ cup (45 g) desiccated coconut |

1  Preheat the oven to 180°C (160°C fan-forced). Line two large baking trays with non-stick baking paper. Using electric beaters, cream the butter and sugar until pale and fluffy, then beat in the egg and vanilla.

2  Gently mix in the sifted flour and the salt. Stir in the hazelnuts, chopped chocolate and coconut until they are evenly combined. Roll the mixture into balls about the size of a walnut and place them on the prepared baking trays, about 6 cm apart to allow for spreading. Flatten them with a fork.

3  Bake for about 12 minutes, until they are just lightly golden around the edges (they will still be soft). Cool them on the trays for a couple of minutes until they firm up slightly, then transfer to a wire rack to cool completely. Store in an airtight container.

*'First things first – put the oven on to preheat, get all the ingredients out to make sure you have everything, grease the tins and get the cooling racks ready before you start.' – Grandma*

# Thelma and Louise's almond biscuits

## makes 20

Preparation time: 15 minutes
Cooking time: 18 minutes

This is a recipe belonging to my friend Louise. It was given to her when she got married, by Thelma, a dear friend of the family. The biscuits are easy to prepare and the decorations can be varied.

| | |
|---|---|
| 60 g butter | 1 egg, lightly beaten |
| 90 g plain flour | 1 tsp almond essence |
| 90 g caster sugar | 10 glacé cherries, to decorate (optional) |
| 120 g ground almonds | |

1  Preheat the oven to 180°C (160°C fan-forced) and line a baking tray with non-stick baking paper. Rub the butter into the flour until they are evenly combined, and then, still using your fingers, mix in the sugar and ground almonds.

2  Add the egg to the flour mixture along with the almond essence. Use a knife to mix them in, then gather the dough together.

3  Take level tablespoons of the dough and, using your hands, mould them into small flat biscuits, about 5 cm in diameter, and place them on the prepared tray. Cut the glacé cherries in half and place one half on top of each biscuit, if desired. Bake for 18 minutes, until lightly golden on top and brown underneath. Transfer to a wire rack to cool.

*'I once complained to my mother that other people served their cakes cold and with icing on them, which I didn't like. Mum explained that she would have iced the cakes but with three boys they never had the chance to cool down before being eaten. My favourite cake is still hot teacake with cinnamon.' – Marcus*

# Speculaas

## makes 24

Preparation time: 20 minutes
Cooking time: about 25 minutes

These speculaas are a traditional Dutch biscuit – another family recipe from my friend Megan, and a childhood favourite of her dad, Burt. Thanks to her mum's efforts to learn these recipes, Megan and her brothers and sisters have grown up with a real sense of both their Dutch and Australian heritage.

3⅓ cups (500 g) plain flour
1 tbs baking powder
1 tsp salt
1 tbs cinnamon
1 tsp ground cloves
1 tsp ground nutmeg

½ tsp white pepper
½ tsp ground aniseed
1¼ cups (250 g) brown sugar
250 g unsalted butter, cubed
¼ cup (60 ml) milk
¼ cup (25 g) flaked almonds

1  Preheat the oven to 220°C (200°C fan-forced) and grease two large baking trays (or line them with non-stick baking paper). Sift the flour, baking powder, salt and spices into a large bowl, then stir in the sugar. Add the butter and rub it into the dry ingredients until the mixture resembles breadcrumbs, then pour in the milk and mix to a supple dough.

2  Gather the dough together and turn it out onto a lightly floured work surface. Roll it out to 2 cm thick, then cut it into 4 cm squares and place them on the prepared trays. Press the almonds into the dough.

3  Bake for 7 minutes, then reduce the heat to 160°C (140°C fan-forced) and bake for a further 20–25 minutes. The cookies are ready when they are nicely brown. Transfer to wire racks to cool before storing in airtight containers.

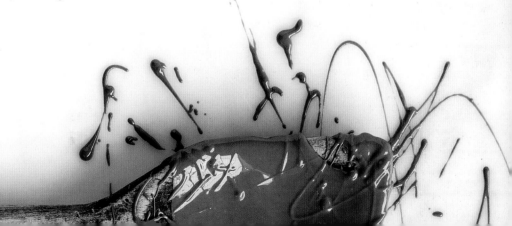

# Grandma's shortbread

## makes about 35

Preparation time: 20 minutes
Cooking time: 8–10 minutes per batch

One of the best remembered treats of Grandma's was her shortbread.
It was a staple of her afternoon tea menu for many years.

250 g unsalted butter
¾ cup (110 g) icing sugar mixture
1 tsp vanilla essence
½ cup (70 g) cornflour

2 cups (300 g) self-raising flour
good pinch of salt
caster sugar, extra, for dipping

1　Preheat the oven to 180°C (160°C fan-forced) and grease two large baking trays. Using electric beaters, beat the butter and icing sugar until light and creamy, then beat in the vanilla essence.

2　Sift the cornflour, self-raising flour and salt together. Add them to the butter mixture and use a butter knife to mix together thoroughly.

3　Roll the dough into small balls about the size of a walnut. Dip the tops in the sugar and put them on the prepared tray, about 5 cm apart. Flatten slightly with a fork.

4　Bake for about 8–10 minutes, or until just starting to colour underneath (the biscuits will still be soft, and pale on top). Leave on the trays for 10 minutes to become firm, then transfer to a wire rack to cool completely. Store in an airtight container.

*Note:* You can make the shortbread larger or smaller, but you will have to adjust the cooking time. It can also be made by pressing the dough into a slice pan and cutting it into squares when cooked but still warm.

*'When mixing cakes, only stir in one direction
or you will unmix them!' – Grandma*

# Nan's pikelets

## makes about 20

........................................................................................

Preparation time: 5 minutes + 30 minutes resting
Cooking time: 15 minutes

The smell of pikelets cooking transports me straight back to Nan's house. They were so often a treat there, and we enjoyed them just cooling, with butter and jam. They are also good cold, with whipped cream and lemon butter, or hot with sugar and lemon juice – but no matter what topping you choose, pikelets should be eaten the day they are made.

1 cup (150 g) self-raising flour        ¾ cup (180 ml) milk
        1 tbs caster sugar        ¼ cup butter, melted
                1 egg

1   Sift the flour and caster sugar into a medium bowl. Lightly beat the egg in a small bowl and add the milk. Make a well in the centre of the dry ingredients and add the wet ingredients, stirring well. Make sure there are no lumps, then cover and let rest for 30 minutes.

2   Brush a large frying pan with butter and drop tablespoons of the mixture into the pan. Only make about six pikelets at a time. Cook over medium heat until bubbles appear over most of the surface of the pikelets.

3   Turn and cook on the other side until golden brown. Serve the pikelets hot or cold, with the topping of your choice.

*'Use good butter and fresh eggs – the better the ingredients,
the better the taste.' – Nan*

# Mum Coughlan's passionfruit shortbread
## makes 8

Preparation time: 20 minutes
Cooking time: 30 minutes

This is truly a secret family recipe – or it was. Held close for a long time by my friends the Coughlan family, they have agreed to share it with me and with you.

125 g unsalted butter, cold, cubed
1⅔ cups (250 g) plain flour
125 g caster sugar
pinch salt
1 egg
1 tsp caster sugar, extra, to sprinkle

**Passionfruit cream**
2 tbs unsalted butter, at room temperature
1 cup (150 g) icing sugar mixture
1½ tbs passionfruit pulp

1  Preheat the oven to 180°C (160°C fan-forced). Grease a 20 cm springform cake tin and line the base with non-stick baking paper. Rub the butter into the flour until it resembles breadcrumbs (make sure your hands are cool). Alternatively, process in a food processor. (I am not sure what Mum Coughlan would make of this, it's my shortcut!) Add the sugar and a pinch of salt, then stir to combine. Mix in the egg with a knife (or process in short bursts) to form a dough, then turn out onto a lightly floured surface and gather it together with your hands.

2  Press the dough into the prepared tin, then rough up the top with a fork and sprinkle it with the extra caster sugar. Bake for 30 minutes, or until a pale golden brown. Cool in the tin for 15 minutes, then release the side and slide off the base and onto a wire rack to cool completely.

3  To make the passionfruit cream, beat the butter and icing sugar using electric beaters, until they are combined. Add the passionfruit pulp a little at a time, mixing well, until the mixture resembles whipped cream.

4  Cut the shortbread into 16 wedges with a very sharp knife. Sandwich two pieces together with the passionfruit cream.

*'Use your fingertips to rub butter into flour for pastry – they are the coolest part of your hands.' – Nan*

Sweet treats

# Treacle scones

## makes about 10

.....................................................

Preparation time: 10 minutes
Cooking time: 7–10 minutes

Scones are very inexpensive, quick and easy to make. This treacle scone recipe is tucked away in my nan's mother's tattered and careworn handwritten recipe book. I like the idea that my children are enjoying a treat made for my nan when she was a child herself.

1⅔ cups (250 g) self-raising flour      2 tbs golden syrup
½ tsp salt      ½ cup (125 ml) milk
3 tsp unsalted butter      1 egg, lightly beaten, to glaze

1   Preheat the oven to 200°C (180°C fan-forced). Sift the flour and salt into a large bowl and make a well in the centre.

2   Place the butter and golden syrup in a small saucepan over medium heat until the syrup is dissolved, then add the milk. Add this mixture to the flour and use a wooden spoon to mix it to a soft dough.

3   Gather the dough together and turn it out onto a lightly floured surface. Knead it very slightly, then press out to 2 cm thickness. Use a 5 or 6 cm cutter to cut it into rounds (get as many as you can from the first cut). Press the offcuts together and cut out more scones.

4   Place the scones on a baking tray, just touching each other, and brush them lightly with the egg. Bake for 10 minutes, until risen and golden. Serve warm, with jam, or the topping of your choice.

Note: These scones are pictured on page 166 with my strawberry and palm sugar jam.

*'Once I was baking a double batch of scones while Mum went to pick my grandparents up. I wasn't sure about cooking times as I hadn't cooked a double batch before. I asked Dad about it, which was probably a mistake, as he was a real joker. He said if it was a double batch they would need to cook for twice as long. Naturally they were horribly burned.' – Marlene*

# Mum Goodwin's chocolate cake

## serves 12

Preparation time: 20 minutes
Cooking time: 35–40 minutes

This one of Grandma's recipes that was baked regularly by Mick's mum, Kathleen. Mick and his brothers and sisters would often enjoy it for afternoon tea. It is fabulous drizzled with chocolate ganache. It can also be made in round tins and iced with chocolate butter icing or sandwiched with raspberry jam. Large muffin tins are another option – just reduce the cooking time to 15 minutes.

1¼ cups (125 g) cocoa powder
1½ cups (375 ml) boiling water
180 g unsalted butter, cubed
2½ cups (550 g) caster sugar
3 eggs

¾ cup (185 ml) milk
2 tsp white vinegar
½ tsp salt
3 cups (450 g) self-raising flour, sifted

1  Preheat the oven to 180°C (160°C fan-forced) and lightly grease a 25 cm bundt tin. Sift the cocoa powder into a bowl and gradually add the boiling water, stirring until smooth, then set aside to cool.

2  Using electric beaters, beat the butter and sugar until light and creamy. Add the eggs one at a time, beating well after each addition. Combine the milk and vinegar in a jug.

3  Add the salt, 1 cup (150 g) of the flour and ¼ cup (60 ml) of the milk to the butter mixture, and stir to combine. Repeat with the remaining flour and milk, then stir in the cocoa mixture and transfer to the prepared tin.

4  Bake for about 35–40 minutes, until the cake springs back when gently touched and pulls away from the sides of the tin. Cool in the tin for 5 minutes, then remove it and place on a wire rack to cool completely before icing.

*Note*: You could bake this mixture in a 26 cm springform tin for 50 minutes, or in three 18 cm sandwich tins for 20–25 minutes.

*'My brothers used to get the mixing bowl after Mum made a chocolate cake. Glen wanted to get the bowl to himself, so he would tell Raymond to whistle. Raymond was very proud that he could whistle, so he would oblige. Glen would say, "Keep whistlin', Bud," until all the cake mix was gone. Raymond fell for it every time.' – Tony*

# Never fail cake

## serves 12

........................................................................................

Preparation time: 20 minutes
Cooking time: 45 minutes

Grandma's 'never fail cake' is as easy to make as the name suggests. It can be done
entirely in an electric mixer, making it quick as well. It's a great stand-by and can
be varied with different flavoured icings or citrus zest added to the batter.

250 g unsalted butter, chopped      3 cups (450 g) self-raising flour
2 cups (440 g) sugar      1½ cups (375 ml) milk
4 eggs      good pinch of salt
½ tsp vanilla essence

1   Preheat the oven to 180°C (160°C fan-forced). Lightly grease a 26 cm springform tin and line
    the base with non-stick baking paper. Using electric beaters, beat the butter and sugar until light
    and creamy. Add the eggs one at a time, beating well between each addition, then beat in the
    vanilla essence.

2   Stir in 1 cup (150 g) of the flour, then ½ cup (125 ml) of the milk. Repeat until all the flour and
    milk is used, and make sure there are no lumps in the batter. Transfer to the prepared cake tin.

3   Bake for about 45 minutes, until the cake springs back when gently touched in the middle and
    comes away from the edges of the pan. Cool in the tin for 5 minutes, then release the sides
    and cool completely on a wire rack before icing with a simple butter frosting.

*Note:* The cake in the photograph is iced with coffee butter cream and decorated with crushed
chocolate-coated coffee beans.

*'Once I went to a friend's place and her mum had cooked a chocolate
cake for dessert. She had hurried it, though, and used Gravox
instead of cocoa. It was awful.' – Debbie*

# Grandma's sponge cake

## serves 8–10

Preparation time: 30 minutes
Cooking time: 22–25 minutes

Grandma was, quite simply, famous for her sponge cake – especially at the Catholic school her children attended. The Brothers who taught there were each baked a cake on their saint's feast day. They would be quite anxious in the lead-up to the day, hoping that the cake would not be forgotten, and sending home not-so-subtle reminders with the children. I suspect that a few of Mick's uncles had an easier ride through high school than they would have if it weren't for the promise of Grandma's sponges.

| | |
|---|---|
| 5 eggs | 500 ml cream |
| pinch salt | 1 tsp vanilla essence |
| 1 cup (220 g) caster sugar | 1 tsp caster sugar, extra |
| ¾ cup (115 g) self-raising flour | ½ cup (125 ml) strawberry jam |
| ½ cup (75 g) cornflour | strawberries or other fruits, to decorate |

1   Preheat the oven to 180°C (160°C fan-forced). Lightly grease two 22½ cm springform cake tins and line the bases with non-stick baking paper.

2   Using electric beaters, beat the eggs at high speed with a pinch of salt, gradually adding the sugar over a couple of minutes. Continue beating for about 10 minutes, until the mixture is pale and fluffy and has increased in volume. Gently fold in the combined sifted flours with a large metal spoon, taking care not to knock the air out of the egg mixture.

3   Pour into the prepared tins. Place both tins on the centre rack of the oven and bake for 22–25 minutes, until they have risen, turned golden and spring back when touched gently in the middle. Carefully run a knife around the edge of each cake and immediately release the sides of the tins. Cool completely. (The cakes may stick to the wire racks once cooled. If so, run a large knife or palette knife underneath to loosen them.)

4   Whip the cream with the vanilla essence and extra sugar. Spread jam over one of the cooled cakes, then spread both cakes with cream and stack them. Decorate with strawberries, passionfruit, grated chocolate, or whatever else you fancy.

*'Sponge mixture should be handled very carefully – tiptoe around it and don't slam the oven door!' – Grandma*

# Sweetheart torte

## serves 8

......................................................................................................

Preparation time: 30 minutes
Cooking time: 40 minutes

What's in a name? When my boys were little I used to introduce them to people as my little darlin's. (They would kill me if I did that now.) I didn't realise how literally they took me until I heard Joe very seriously asking a friend of mine, 'How many darlin's do you have?' I don't know the origin of the intriguing name of this cake but whatever it is, the meringue on top and sweet cake base make it something to bake for your sweetheart – or your little darlin's.

60 g unsalted butter, chopped

1 cup (220 g) caster sugar

2 eggs, separated

½ tsp vanilla essence

1 cup (150 g) plain flour

1½ tsp baking powder

½ tsp salt

⅓ cup (80 ml) milk

¼ tsp cream of tartar

¼ cup (40 g) chopped blanched almonds

2 tsp caster sugar, extra

¼ tsp cinnamon

1   Preheat the oven to 180°C (160°C fan-forced). Grease a 20 cm round springform tin and line the base with non-stick baking paper. Using electric beaters, beat the butter with half the caster sugar until light and creamy. Add the egg yolks and vanilla and beat until combined.

2   Sift the flour, baking powder and salt together, then fold into the butter mixture in two batches, alternating with the milk. Spread into the prepared cake tin.

3   Using electric beaters, beat the eggwhites and cream of tartar until soft peaks form. Gradually add the remaining caster sugar, beating constantly until it is combined and the mixture is thick and glossy.

4   Spread the meringue over the cake batter. Combine the almonds, extra sugar and cinnamon and sprinkle them over the meringue, then swirl with a knife. Bake for about 40 minutes, until the meringue has risen and is lightly browned. When it is done, a skewer or knife inserted into the cake should come out clean. Cool slightly, then run a knife around the edge of the tin before releasing the sides. Cool on a wire rack.

# Burnt sugar cake

## serves 12

Preparation time: 35 minutes
Cooking time: 1 hour 5 minutes

This cake is moist and decadent, with a rich caramel sauce poured over it just before serving.
It is one of my friend Helene's family recipes, given to her by her aunt.

| | |
|---|---|
| 1¾ cups (385 g) caster sugar | **Topping** |
| 125 g unsalted butter, cubed | 2 cups (400 g) brown sugar |
| 2 eggs, separated | 125 g butter |
| 1 tsp vanilla essence | 1 tsp vanilla essence |
| 2½ cups (375 g) plain flour | ½ cup (125 ml) milk |
| 2½ tsp baking powder | pinch of salt |
| good pinch of salt | ½ cup (75 g) chopped, roasted, unsalted cashews |
| 1 cup (250 ml) milk | |

1   Preheat the oven to 180°C (160°C fan-forced). Grease a 23 cm round cake tin and line the base
with non-stick baking paper. Place ¼ cup (55 g) of the caster sugar in a medium saucepan. Cook over
medium heat until melted and dark brown – swirl the pan to distribute the sugar occasionally, but
don't stir. Standing back, carefully add ¼ cup (60 ml) boiling water (watch out – it will spit), then stir
over medium heat until the toffee dissolves. Transfer to a heat-proof jug and set aside to cool.

2   Using electric beaters, beat the butter and remaining sugar until light and creamy. Add the egg yolks
and vanilla essence and beat until combined. Sift the flour, baking powder and salt together, then fold
into the butter mixture in two batches, alternating with the milk. Fold in the cooled sugar syrup.

3   Beat the eggwhites until stiff peaks form and fold them into the batter. Pour into the prepared
tin and bake for about 50 minutes, until the cake springs back when touched gently in the middle.
Turn out onto a wire rack and cool completely.

4   To make the topping, combine all the ingredients except the cashews in a saucepan and stir over
low heat until melted and smooth. Increase the heat to medium, bring to the boil and cook for
10 minutes, until it reaches soft ball stage on a sugar thermometer. Remove from the heat and cool
slightly for 2 minutes. Transfer the mixture to a heat-proof bowl and stand it on a damp kitchen
cloth. Using electric beaters, beat on low speed for 3–4 minutes, until the mixture has thickened
slightly and is lighter in colour. Pour it over the cake, spreading it so it runs down the sides a little.
You have to work quickly, as the topping sets fast. Immediately sprinkle the top with the cashews,
and leave to cool slightly before serving.

# Lemon Diva cupcakes

## makes 12

Preparation time: 30 minutes
Cooking time: 20 minutes

I made these little cupcakes in a MasterChef mystery box challenge. Our brief was to create and name a signature cupcake. I went with a very strong lemon-flavoured cake and named it the Lemon Diva. I was thrilled to pieces to win the challenge and I now get requests to bake them all the time. The secret to the strong lemon flavour is not only plenty of zest in the batter, but lemon juice in the icing as well.

100 g unsalted butter, softened
¾ cup (165 g) caster sugar
½ tsp vanilla extract
finely grated zest of 3 lemons
2 eggs
1⅓ cups (200 g) self-raising flour
½ cup (125 ml) milk

**Icing**
125 g unsalted butter, softened
2 cups (300 g) icing sugar mixture
1½ tbs lemon juice
yellow food colouring (optional)
yellow liquorice allsorts, to decorate

1   Preheat the oven to 180°C (160°C fan-forced). Line a 12-hole medium muffin pan (⅓ cup capacity) with paper cases. Using electric beaters, beat the butter, sugar and vanilla extract until light and creamy. Mix through the lemon zest.

2   Add the eggs one at a time, beating well after each egg. Gently fold through the flour and milk in two alternate batches. Divide the mixture evenly among the paper cases.

3   Bake for about 20 minutes, or until golden brown and springy when touched. Remove from the oven and transfer to a wire rack to cool completely before decorating.

4   To make the icing, use electric beaters to beat the butter until light and creamy. Add the icing sugar a little at a time, beating constantly. Add half the lemon juice and beat until well combined. Add the remaining lemon juice a little at a time, and tint with food colouring if you like. Using a 1 cm fluted nozzle, pipe the icing onto the cooled cupcakes. Decorate with a small lemon shape cut from a yellow piece of liquorice allsort.

*Note*: To make Lime Sublime cupcakes, substitute the zest of 6 limes in the cake batter and 2 tbs of lime juice in the icing. For Clockwork Orange cupcakes, try using the zest of 2 oranges in the batter and 2 tbs of orange juice in the icing.

# 7 | Rainy day cooking

Jams, chutneys and condiments are not something I would whip up on a busy weeknight – that's the sort of task I love to spend a whole day doing. Preferably a rainy, miserable day with the kettle on the boil and not much else going on.

In years past, relishes and sauces of all kinds were made at home, both to use surplus produce from backyard gardens and to save money. Let's face it – making these things is no longer a necessity, as there is such a dizzying abundance of them available in the supermarket, many of them inexpensive. And yet I get so much satisfaction from it.

My jams taste better than mass-produced store-bought preserves, but it's more than that. The stirring, the measuring, the sedate pace of this type of cookery induces that calm serenity that I call my Happy Cooking Place. It gives me a real sense of connection to the generations of women (they are women, for the most part), who have done all this before me and whose handwritten recipes I often work from.

Although far fewer people grow their own produce now than in years past, there is still surplus to be found. On the New South Wales Central Coast, where I live, citrus fruit grows with no effort at all, and we wind up with a glut of gorgeous juicy oranges and lemons every winter. There is a point during the summer each year, too, when tomatoes are ridiculously cheap – so even if you don't grow your own, you can still take advantage of their peak season and 'put up' some lovely chutney or spaghetti sauce.

The sense of accomplishment that comes from seeing a row of shiny labelled jars, filled with a delicious jam or relish, is probably hopelessly old-fashioned. But there it is.

# Basil and cashew pesto

## makes 3 cups

Preparation time: 10 minutes
No cooking time

This pesto can be used as a dip, or is lovely tossed through freshly made pasta. It only takes minutes to prepare. To control the amount of salt in the pesto I prefer to use unsalted nuts. If you buy your cashews raw, roast them in the oven for about 7 minutes at 180°C (160°C fan-forced), until they are golden, and cool before using. You can substitute toasted pine nuts for the cashews if you wish, but they only take 3–4 minutes in the oven – watch them carefully!

200 g roasted unsalted cashew nuts
3 cups basil leaves, loosely packed
(about 2 good-sized bunches)
150 g parmesan, grated

6 cloves garlic, roasted
finely grated zest of ½ lemon
1½ cups (375 ml) olive oil
salt and ground white pepper, to taste

1 Put the cashews, basil, parmesan, garlic and lemon zest into a blender or food processor and blitz until all ingredients are roughly chopped.

2 With the motor running, add the oil gradually, until the mixture is combined but still a little bit chunky. For a dip, you may like to use slightly less oil. Taste and season as desired. If it's not going to be used within a few days, put it in a bowl or container and pour a little olive oil over the top to seal it from the air. Pesto will keep in an airtight container in the fridge for up to three months.

*Note*: To roast garlic, place a whole head on a tray, and bake in the oven at 180°C (160°C fan-forced) for 10 minutes or until soft and fragrant. Cool before using. The roasted garlic will just ooze out of its skin when squeezed. Use as much as necessary for the recipe and store the rest in an airtight container in the fridge for up to a month.

Lime Aïoli

Basil & Cashew
Pesto

# Mayonnaise

## Makes about 2 cups

Preparation time: 10 minutes
No cooking time

Mayo is just nicer when it's homemade. There are two schools of thought about making your own mayonnaise. Some swear by the hand-beaten method; others prefer to use a food processor. I use a food processor, only because I'm not coordinated enough to beat the eggs, hold the bowl and pour the oil in a steady stream all at once. It's still lovely to eat.

3 egg yolks
1 tbs vinegar
1 cup (250 ml) extra light olive oil

salt and ground white pepper, to taste
up to 2 tbs lemon juice

1 Place the egg yolks and vinegar into a food processor and switch it on. Add the olive oil a few drops at a time. When the mixture begins to thicken, add the oil in a steady flow until it is all incorporated.

2 Season with salt and pepper, and add lemon juice to your taste. Keep in the fridge for up to a week.

# Lime aioli

makes 2 cups

Preparation time: 10 minutes
No cooking time

Perfect for a seafood dipping sauce, this lovely tangy aioli has pride of place on the Christmas table alongside the fresh king prawns, sea salt and lime cheeks.

¼ cup (60 ml) Dijon mustard

¼ cup (60 ml) lime juice

2 garlic cloves, crushed

3 egg yolks

300 ml olive oil

salt, to taste

1   Place the mustard, lime juice, garlic and egg yolks into a blender or food processor and blend.

2   With the motor running, add the olive oil a couple of drops at a time and blend well after each addition. The mixture will begin to thicken or emulsify. When this happens the oil can be added a little more quickly, until all of it has been incorporated.

3   Taste and season with salt, then keep in the fridge for up to a week.

# Eggplant mustard pickle

## makes about 3 cups

Preparation time: 20 minutes + 1 hour standing
Cooking time: about 20 minutes

This is one of my friend Helene's recipes. It goes beautifully with the other
Sri Lankan dishes in this book. It packs quite a punch – not for the faint-hearted!

| | |
|---|---|
| 2 large eggplants (about 900 g) | **Mustard mixture** |
| 2 tsp turmeric | ½ cup (90 g) mustard seeds |
| 2 tsp salt | ¼ cup (60 ml) white vinegar (plus a little more) |
| oil for frying | 4 garlic cloves, halved |
| | 5 cm piece ginger, peeled and chopped |
| | 1 tbs chilli powder |
| | 1 tbs salt |
| | 2 tsp sugar |

1   Cut the eggplant into 1.5 cm cubes, then place it in a bowl with the turmeric and salt and toss it through until it is coated. Cover the eggplant with cold water and put a plate over it to keep it submerged. Leave it standing for 1 hour, then drain and pat dry with paper towels.

2   Meanwhile, place all the mustard mixture ingredients into a blender or food processor and blend or process until smooth.

3   Pour 2–3 cm of oil into a deep frying pan or wok and cook the eggplant in batches until it is golden. Make sure not to overcrowd the pan while frying. Remove the eggplant with a slotted spoon and drain it on paper towels.

4   Heat 1 tbs of oil in a large frying pan and fry 3 tbs of the mustard mixture. Add extra vinegar to give the mustard mixture a runny consistency and then stir in the sugar. (If you prefer a sweeter pickle, add a little more sugar.) Add the eggplant and stir gently until it is thoroughly coated with the mustard mixture.

5   Serve at room temperature as a side dish or condiment. The pickle will keep in an airtight container in the fridge for up to 4 months.

*Note*: The mustard mixture makes about 3 times as much as you need for this recipe. It will keep in the fridge for up to 6 months.

# Curried mango chutney

## makes 4–5 cups

Preparation time: 20 minutes
Cooking time: 40 minutes

Mangoes, to me, are the very essence of summer. I buy them by the box in the weeks leading up to Christmas and fill the house with their rich, sweet aroma. If I'm going to make my mango chutney I have to warn the boys off the fruit or they will eat the lot. As well as being a great accompaniment to curries and rice, this chutney is delicious on sandwiches, burgers and cold meats. It is sweet with a bit of a hot bite to it.

¼ cup (60 ml) olive oil
1 tsp sambal oelek or crushed chilli
¼ cup (60 g) freshly grated ginger
1 garlic clove, crushed
1 onion, diced
½ red capsicum, diced

1 kg mango flesh, roughly chopped (see note)
150 ml pineapple juice
200 ml white wine vinegar
¾ cup (150 g) brown sugar
2 tbs curry powder
⅔ cup (120 g) raisins

1   Heat the olive oil in a chef's pan or large deep frying pan and add the sambal oelek. Stir for a minute over medium heat until it is fragrant. Add the ginger, garlic, onion and capsicum and sauté for 3 minutes, then add the mango and turn off the heat.

2   Combine the pineapple juice, vinegar, sugar and curry powder in a bowl. Mix well and add to the pan, along with the raisins, then bring the mixture to the boil. Reduce to a simmer and cook for about 30 minutes, until reduced and thickened.

3   Pour the hot mixture into warm sterilised jars and seal. Cool, label and date, then keep in the fridge for up to 3 months.

Note: You will need 4 large mangoes for this recipe (about 1.6 kg before peeling and pitting). Choose fruit that is ripe and fragrant.

# Tomato relish

## makes about 4 cups

Preparation time: 10 minutes
Cooking time: 1½ hours

We planted a vegetable patch last year and made all the errors that novices make – among them, planting everything at once, and all too close together, so the garden was a wild riot of greenery. When the vegetables came in they came all at once – we had kilos and kilos of zucchinis and cucumbers and thousands of tomatoes, all at the same time.

This season we swore to be more sensible, to plant in cycles and follow instructions. And so we did. However, every seed from every tomato that fell to the ground last season has sprouted, and once again, our garden looks like a jungle rather than an orderly vegetable patch.

I guarantee this year that the tomato relish recipe is going to get a workout.

1 tbs olive oil
2 tbs curry powder
¼ tsp cayenne pepper
500 g onions, thinly sliced
2 kg ripe red tomatoes, chopped

1 tsp sea salt
1 cup (250 ml) white wine vinegar
375 g brown sugar
2 tbs wholegrain mustard

1   Heat the olive oil in a large pot over medium-high heat, then add the curry powder and cayenne pepper. Stir for a minute, until fragrant. Add the onions and cook for a further minute, then add the tomatoes and bring to the boil.

2   Add the rest of the ingredients. Lower the heat and simmer uncovered for 1 hour, or until reduced to a thick, spreadable consistency. Taste and add more sugar or salt if you think it needs it.

3   Spoon into sterilised jars and seal. Keep in the fridge for up to 6 months.

# Red onion jam

## makes about 3 cups

·······································································

Preparation time: 15 minutes
Cooking time: 30 minutes

This savoury jam is delicious served on a cheese platter, with sausages, or as a chutney on cold meat sandwiches. For a simple finger food for parties, spoon it into small cooked pastry shells (either homemade or bought), and crumble in a little goats' cheese.

| | |
|---|---|
| 1 tbs olive oil | 1 cup (250 ml) red wine vinegar |
| 6 large or 8 medium red onions | ½ cup (110 g) caster sugar |
| (about 1.5 kg), sliced very finely | salt, to taste |

1   Heat the olive oil in a chef's pan or a large, deep frying pan over medium-low heat. Add the onions and sweat them gently until they are soft, translucent and collapsed. This should take about 10 minutes, depending on the size of the pan. Make sure they don't brown at all.

2   Stir in the vinegar and sugar – the onions will turn a beautiful magenta colour. Simmer, stirring occasionally, until the liquid reduces and the onions have the consistency of a jam or chutney. Season to taste.

3   Cool, then transfer to a jar or bowl. The jam will set in the fridge. Cover and keep for up to 3 weeks. Before using, warm it up a little in the microwave or on the stovetop.

*Note:* For me this jam usually takes about twenty minutes to reach setting point, but others following the same recipe have found it takes up to an hour. Results seem to vary according to the equipment you use, so save your first attempt at this jam for a slow rainy day at home.

# Strawberry and palm sugar jam

## makes 2 cups

Preparation time: 10 minutes
Cooking time: 20 minutes

I first made this jam by accident, under pressure in the MasterChef kitchen. I had forgotten to get caster sugar from the pantry and was not allowed to go back for it. Luckily I had palm sugar for another recipe, so I decided to give it a go. The palm sugar imparts a subtle caramel flavour to the jam and, for some reason that I don't understand, also seems to act as a setting agent.

500 g strawberries, halved      500 g palm sugar, grated
water, as needed

1   Place the strawberries in a saucepan and stir them over medium heat with a spatula. Add trickles of water if they start to stick to the pot.

2   Add the palm sugar and stir to dissolve, adding tiny amounts of water if necessary. Bring to the boil and boil rapidly for around 12 minutes, or until the jam reaches setting point. To test, spread a teaspoonful on a cold saucer. Let it cool in the fridge for a couple of minutes, then push it with your finger – if it wrinkles, it is the right consistency.

3   Pour the hot mixture into warm sterilised jars and seal. Cool, label and date, then keep in the fridge for up to 6 months.

# Orange jam

## makes 2 cups

Preparation time: 30 minutes + overnight soaking
Cooking time: 1 hour 50 minutes

I have never been a fan of orange marmalade, because I dislike big chunky pieces of peel.
This jam has very fine peel, so you get all the orange flavour without the bitter chunky bits.

| | |
|---|---|
| 500 g oranges | 1 kg caster sugar |
| 1.2 litres water | juice of 1 lemon |

1   Using a zester, finely shred the orange zest from the fruit and set it aside. Cut the pith off the oranges and discard it, then finely chop the orange flesh, removing and reserving the pips. Tie the pips into a piece of muslin cloth. If you don't have muslin, the cheat's alternative is to empty out an unused teabag, put the pips in, and tie it up with its own string.

2   Combine the zest, orange flesh, water and pips in a large pot with a lid and soak them overnight.

3   The next day, bring the mixture to a slow simmer and cook for about 1½ hours, until the orange zest is very soft.

4   Take out the bag of pips and then stir in the sugar and the lemon juice, without boiling, until the sugar has dissolved. Bring to the boil and cook rapidly, uncovered, for about 20 minutes, until the mixture reaches setting point. To test, spread a teaspoonful on a cold saucer. Let it cool in the fridge for a couple of minutes, then push it with your finger – if it wrinkles, it is the right consistency.

5   Pour the hot mixture into warm sterilised jars and seal. Cool, label and date, then keep in the fridge for up to 6 months.

*Note:* If you are using oranges with no pips, take the pips from your lemon. The pips provide pectin, which helps to set the jam.

# Lemon butter

## makes 2 cups

..................................................................................

Preparation time: 5 minutes
Cooking time: 20 minutes

As a spread for sponge cake, a filling for tarts, slathered on bread or just eaten out of the jar with a spoon, there's not much better than this old school fete favourite.

4 eggs, lightly beaten            ½ cup (125 ml) lemon juice
1 cup (220 g) caster sugar        125 g butter, cubed

1   Place the eggs and sugar in a bowl over a saucepan of barely simmering water and whisk until the sugar dissolves.

2   Add the lemon juice and butter and whisk constantly for around 20 minutes, or until the mixture thickens. Do not allow it to get too hot or to boil.

3   Pour the warm mixture into sterilised jars and seal. Keep in the fridge for up to a week.

Lemon Butter

# Passionfruit butter

## makes about 4 cups

Preparation time: 15 minutes
Cooking time: 25 minutes

Just like lemon butter, this passionfruit butter has many uses. It is lovely in little individual tarts or as a spread for cakes or biscuits. This recipe makes a large amount, the idea being to put up a few jars and give some to the neighbours. Passionfruit vines are very easy to grow and don't take up much space in the garden, so it's worth giving them a try.

375 g butter
750 g caster sugar

pulp of 18 passionfruit
6 eggs, lightly beaten

1  Place the butter and sugar in a large saucepan and stir over medium heat until the butter has melted and the mixture is combined. Add the passionfruit pulp and stir to dissolve the sugar. Remove from the heat and cool for 10 minutes.

2  Reduce the heat to very low and quickly whisk in the eggs. Stir continuously with a whisk for about 15 minutes, until the mixture thickens. Be careful not to overheat the mixture or it will curdle.

3  Pour the warm mixture into sterilised jars and seal. Keep in the fridge for up to a week.

One of Mick's mates from high school, also called Mick, married Kylie, a lovely lady who keeps him in line and who comes from an Italian background. They live just around the corner from us now, and our kids play together. When Kylie was small she used to make tomato sauce with her family every summer.

'When tomatoes were in season, Pop would take his truck to the fruit and veg markets before dawn on the Saturday and buy a truckload. He would return around seven am and that's when the bottling took place. The double garage was reinvented as a tomato bottling factory with hundreds of empty longneck beer bottles ready to be used.

'The bottles had been sterilised and it was the grandchildren's job to stuff two basil leaves in each bottle. The tomatoes were put through a mincer, which separated the skin, and the tomato juice was then poured into each bottle. Once all the bottles were full they were sealed and put into big gallon drums and boiled up for around two hours. That was it – we all then had fresh tomato sauce to use for pasta for the next twelve months.

'It was a really fun time and involved all family members, no matter how old or young. Nonna would disappear around lunchtime and reappear with her famous antipasti platters with fresh bread rolls for lunch.

'It amazes me when I look back how daggy I thought this all was, but I would now give anything for my kids to experience it – it's a shame that the old ways die off with each generation.'

# 8 | Wide *open* spaces

Some of the best summer holidays I had as a kid were in the camping ground of a little town called Dalmeny. The campground there had no power and basic amenities, but it sat, as it still does, proudly perched on a hillside overlooking the ocean. The campers became a kind of community. We would sit around our camp fires, and on New Years' Eve at midnight we'd bang our pots and pans and wander around to the other fires to say Happy New Year.

I will never forget one particular camping trip, the only one we ever bailed out of. We had gone to Wombeyan Caves for the June long weekend. We rugged up as best we could before going to bed; Mum even strapped space blankets over us so they wouldn't fall off. It became so bitterly cold in the tent during the night that we all wound up sleeping in the car. When I woke up in the morning, I was squashed up against the tailgate of the station wagon. All the condensation had run down the inside wall of the car, and I had a crispy coasting of ice over my sleeping bag. I had ice in my eyebrows and eyelashes, too. I don't remember ever being so cold before or since. We later learned that it was ⁻4°C. We decided to have a hot shower to get the circulation going again, but the water had frozen in the pipes. This was the last straw and Mum declared the camping trip over. We left a day early – none of us complained.

Mick and I now love to go camping with our boys. Sometimes just our family heads off, sometimes we join other families. We have camped very rough, and also in some nice resort-style caravan parks. My favourite kind of camping is where we can light a fire. There is something primitive and compelling about a fire that draws people in.

I love the simplicity of camping. It's a reminder of how little we actually need to survive. Of how enjoyable life can be when it's stripped right back to the basics. I also love that some of the most delicious food can be cooked without a kitchen, with only rudimentary equipment and ingredients. After a day exploring, fossicking, swimming and generally running wild, simple warming food cooked over an open flame tastes like manna from heaven. Some of my best memories are centred around the camp fire, and I hope my children can say the same thing when they grow up.

# Wayne's camp oven roasted pork

## serves 6–8

Preparation time: 10 minutes
Cooking time: approximately 1 hour

Wayne was my mother-in-law's neighbour for many years. He often takes his two sons and goes bush. He is our version of the bush tucker man. Wayne says cooking in the camp oven is just as easy as cooking in the kitchen: 'For roasts, allow about an hour a kilo. The main trick is keeping the meat moist. You could use pork shoulder or rolled leg instead of a rolled loin roast, if you like – just take note of the weight when you buy it and adjust the cooking time accordingly.'

1 tbs white vinegar
rolled pork loin roast (about 1 kg)

2 tsp coarse sea salt
375 ml bottle cider (sweet or dry)

1 Light a fire and let it burn down to glowing hot coals. Place the camp oven on the coals and place some coals on the lid, so it heats up.

2 Rub the vinegar into the pork rind and then rub in the salt. Place the pork onto a trivet in the camp oven and carefully pour the cider into the base of the oven. Put the lid back on and cook for about 30 minutes. Uncover and check the rind – if it is getting very brown and crackling nicely, take the coals off the lid to finish cooking. If not, leave the coals on the lid a bit longer and check again later. The pork will need to be cooked for 1 hour per kilogram. If yours weighs more than a kilo, calculate the extra time it will need.

3 When it is ready, remove the pork from the camp oven. Set aside on a plate, loosely covered with foil, and let it rest for at least 15 minutes before slicing.

*'One of my favourite things about camping is settling in to a good tasty meal. I love cooking around the fire. It's the heart of any camp – it's where the cooking and the socialising go on.' – Wayne*

# Steve's barbecued lamb leg

## serves 8

Preparation time: 15 minutes + marinating
Cooking time: 30 minutes

Before my sister-in-law Liz married her husband, Steve, he had to meet the approval of her four protective brothers. I think his barbecued lamb leg may have been one of the persuading factors.

2 tsp fennel seeds
2 tsp coriander seeds
2 tsp dried chilli flakes
finely chopped stems from
1 bunch coriander

2 tbs Dijon mustard
1.5 kg deboned, butterflied
lamb leg or shoulder

1   Place the spices into a dry frying pan and cook over medium heat for about a minute, until fragrant and toasted. Cool, then grind in a mortar and pestle. Combine with the coriander stems and mustard.

2   Score the meat and smear the mustard mixture all over. Place in a plastic bag and refrigerate for a few hours, or overnight if possible.

3   Take the meat out of the fridge about 1 hour before cooking. Preheat a covered barbecue to medium (about 180°C if you have a gauge). Place the meat on the grill and put the lid down, then cook for 30 minutes, turning once. It should have a lovely blackened and caramelised surface, and be pink and juicy inside the thickest parts.

4   Rest the meat for 15 minutes, then cut into chunky strips. Serve with pita bread, salad, couscous, salsa or whatever you like.

Note: If you don't have a covered barbecue you can place a large foil baking dish over the meat as it cooks. Ask your butcher to debone and butterfly the lamb for you.

*'Balsamic vinegar never goes astray at a barbecue. Pour it over the onions while they are cooking, or on tomatoes with cayenne pepper and sea salt.' – Leon*

# Camp fire side dishes

'Don't try to wash the hotplate in the dishwasher.' – Kyle

### Barbecue appetiser
Soak bamboo skewers in water for about 20 minutes, then thread a slice of chorizo sausage and a slice of haloumi cheese lengthways onto them. Cook on the hotplate for about a minute each side. Top each skewer with half a cherry tomato and serve straight away.

### Frog's eyes
A camping breakfast favourite. Use an egg ring to cut a hole in a piece of bread, then place it on a hot barbecue plate and crack an egg into the hole. Cook, flipping over halfway through. Cook the round piece of bread at the same time, in bacon fat or butter, and serve it on top.

### Camp fire jacket potatoes
Wrap washed potatoes in foil and bury them in the coals of the fire until you can pierce them with a knife. Serve with sour cream or butter.

### Barbecued pineapple
Carve up a fresh pineapple and throw it on the grill with a scattering of sugar and cinnamon for a barbecue dessert. Serve with ice-cream from the esky.

### Vegetable kebabs
Soak bamboo skewers in water for about 20 minutes, then thread them with your favourite vegetables – chunky pieces of capsicum, onion, squash, eggplant, mushrooms, zucchini – whatever takes your fancy. Drizzle with olive oil and put them on the barbie, then brush them with teriyaki sauce or your favourite marinade as they cook.

### Corn on the cob
Peel back the green husk, remove the silk, and rub with butter, salt and pepper. Wrap the husk back around the corn and put it on the hotplate for 10 minutes or so, turning occasionally, until tender.

# Thai pork salad

## serves 4

Preparation time: 30 minutes + 1 hour marinating
Cooking time: about 10 minutes + 5–10 minutes resting

Despite the number of ingredients, this is a really easy and delicious salad. The preparation can be done earlier so the meat can just be quickly cooked on the barbecue or grill when it's time to eat.

1 tbs peanut oil
2 garlic cloves, crushed
2 cm piece ginger, peeled and finely grated
1 small red chilli, deseeded and finely chopped
500 g pork fillet
100 g mixed salad leaves
1 Lebanese cucumber, deseeded and julienned very finely
1 carrot, julienned very finely
½ red capsicum, julienned very finely

1 red onion, sliced very finely
1 tsp peanut oil, extra
1 tbs fresh lime juice
2 tbs sweet chilli sauce
2 tsp fish sauce
1 cup (50 g) bean sprouts
2 bunches coriander, leaves picked
2 bunches mint, leaves picked, and torn if large
¼ cup (40 g) salted peanuts, chopped

1   Combine the peanut oil, garlic, ginger and chilli in a bowl. Toss the pork fillets through the marinade. Cover and refrigerate for 1 hour.

2   Arrange the salad leaves on a large platter or 4 individual serving plates, and top with the cucumber, carrot, capsicum and red onion. Combine the extra peanut oil, lime juice and sauces in a glass jug or bowl.

3   Preheat a barbecue or chargrill pan to high. Sear the pork on each side for about 2–3 minutes. Move to a cooler part of the plate, or reduce the heat slightly, and continue to cook for a further 5–6 minutes, turning occasionally, or until only slightly pink in the middle. Cooking time will vary depending on how thick the fillets are. To test whether they are cooked, pierce the thickest part with a skewer. The juices should run clear.

4   Rest the meat for 5–10 minutes after cooking, then slice finely across the grain. Arrange over the salad. Scatter with the bean sprouts, coriander, mint and peanuts, then drizzle the dressing over the top.

# Camp fire train smash

## Serves 4

.........................................................................................

Preparation time: 15 minutes
Cooking time: 15 minutes

Train smash vegetables are so named because they look like, well, a train smash. This dish comes from Mick's uncles and cousins, the Heneberys. They are campers from way back and know how to rustle up a great meal on the fire. This is a very simple vegetable dinner to make when camping. It minimises the washing-up but maximises the flavour.

| | |
|---|---|
| 2 tbs olive or vegetable oil | 1 eggplant, chopped (optional) |
| 1 onion, coarsely chopped | 250 g mushrooms, halved |
| 2 garlic cloves, chopped | 400 g can chopped tomatoes |
| 2 zucchini, sliced or coarsely chopped | 1 bunch asparagus, trimmed (optional) |
| 1 red capsicum, chopped | salt and freshly ground black pepper, to taste |
| 4 button squash, quartered (optional) | |

1   Heat the oil in a large billy can, saucepan or frying pan and add the onion and garlic. Cook until soft. Add the zucchini, capsicum, squash and eggplant and cook until they are soft, then add the mushrooms, tomatoes and asparagus.

2   Cook until all the vegies soften and the flavour develops. Season with salt and pepper.

*'Barbecues at Mick's are BYO – Bring Your Own fire extinguisher. Occasionally it's BYO barbecue gas. We all stand around the hotplate with a beer. Not for drinking, but to douse the flames.' – Adam*

*'We call Mick the Lord of Flame. He manages to create some pretty special pyrotechnic displays out of a bit of sausage fat. We especially like the charred effect on the ceiling of the barbecue area.' – Daniel*

*'I consider it prudent to have a fire blanket handy in the very rare and unforeseeable event of a fire.' – Mick*

# Wayne's camp fire risotto

## serves 8–10 as an accompaniment

Preparation time: 15 minutes
Cooking time: about 30 minutes

This is another of Wayne's camp fire classics. He explains: 'A favourite side dish that goes with any steak or snags is lemon risotto. Cooking risotto ties you to the fire (which is a good thing if the esky is close) and the social chatter revolves around the cook. This will serve a large family as a side to any meat. If you want to go vegetarian, try adding some fresh or frozen peas, carrot and/or broccoli close to the end of cooking.'

| | |
|---|---|
| 6 cups (1.5 litres) chicken stock | 2 cups (440 g) arborio rice |
| 2 tbs olive oil | ¾ cup (185 ml) white wine |
| 1 large onion, diced | juice and finely grated zest of 1 large lemon |
| 4 cloves garlic, chopped | 2½ cups (200 g) finely grated parmesan |
| 80 g butter | |

1  Put the chicken stock in a pot and heat until it is just at a near simmer (I admit to using stock cubes and river water when camping but prefer homemade stock at home). Heat the oil in a very large saucepan and cook the onion and garlic until soft and golden brown. Add the butter, and when it has melted, add the rice.

2  Stir until well and truly coated in the butter mixture, then add the wine. When this begins to simmer, add enough of the hot stock to cover the rice. As it simmers, keep adding stock so that the rice is always covered. Stir or agitate the pot occasionally so the rice cooks evenly and doesn't catch on the bottom.

3  Taste the rice often after 15–20 minutes. If it's just about cooked, stop adding stock and allow the liquid to reduce. When it's just about fully reduced, add the lemon juice and zest and stir in the parmesan. Set the risotto aside to rest and absorb the juice for a few minutes before serving.

*'The Tong Master has the absolute authority over the food on the barbecue and no one is allowed to so much as turn a sausage, unless they are either ceremoniously handed the tongs, or given permission by the Tong Master.' – Brian*

# Anthony's sautéed tomatoes on the barbecue

## serves 4–6

.................................................................................

Preparation time: 15 minutes
Cooking time: about 10 minutes

Most blokes I know are proud of their prowess on the barbie, and Anthony,
one of the IT consultants who works for our family business, is no exception. This dish
is one of his regulars. Quantities and even ingredients can be varied depending
on the number of guests and personal preference.

5–6 Roma tomatoes, chopped
1 onion, chopped
4–6 rashers rindless shortcut bacon, chopped

handful button mushrooms, sliced (about 150 g)
a good drizzle of extra-virgin olive oil

1  Preheat a barbecue flat plate to medium. Place the ingredients in a bowl and drizzle with the
olive oil. Mix so that everything is coated in oil. Turn onto the barbecue plate and cook until
brown and heated through.

2  Season with salt and freshly ground black pepper. Don't overcook, or it will go mushy.

*'When barbecuing, if you do not have a cold beverage in one*
*hand and tongs in the other, you are not doing it right.' – Anthony*

*'I always cook spuds wrapped in foil in the camp fire coals and I always overcook the*
*sausages. The fire must be cool enough to cook on so it needs to burn down to coals at*
*least in parts. It is customary to drink beer while waiting for the fire to cool down.*
*I recommend starting with a very big fire.' – Vince*

*'Too many cooks spoil the broth. Not that you would cook broth*
*on the barbecue, necessarily.' – Andrew*

# Damper on a stick

## makes about 8

Preparation time: 15 minutes
Cooking time: about 10 minutes

Damper is traditionally made with only flour and water and you can certainly give that a go if you're game. But I am spoiled and like the extra ingredients. These dampers are made on a stick. If you're worried about the cleanliness of this, cover the stick with foil, but be warned – it may be tricky to remove. I don't recall being worried as a kid – we ate them bark and all. It's camping – it's meant to be a bit rough.

4 cups (600 g) self-raising flour
1 tsp salt
100 g butter, cubed

2 cups (500 ml) milk
butter and golden syrup, to serve

1   Send the kids off to find eight sticks, about 3–4 cm thick, and long enough to hold over the fire without burning yourself! Mix the flour and salt together, then rub the butter through with your fingertips. Add almost all the milk and then mix to form a soft dough, adding the rest of the milk if you think you need it.

2   Divide the dough into eight portions and roll them into long snakes. Wind a snake around the end of each stick, pressing the coils together to make sure there are no gaps. You should also make sure the dough isn't too thick, or it will burn on the outside before it cooks on the inside.

3   The tips of the flames are the hottest part of the fire, so don't hold your damper there or it will burn quickly. Instead, find a little cave of coals near the base of the fire. Hold the damper over the coals until it's golden brown and crunchy all over, then carefully remove it from the stick. Put a knob of butter and some golden syrup into the hole and eat it while it's hot. Yum!

My mum, Marlene, grew up in Ryde, Sydney, with an older brother, Barry, my nan, Edna, and my poppy, Roy. Although not a wealthy family in monetary terms, they had a philosophy of good living that they always adhered to: good friends, good times, music, food, travel. Mum tells the story . . .

'Caravans were a new concept in 1939. Dad built ours – he was a carpenter. We would go to Narrabeen or Palm Beach on a Friday afternoon and stay until around 6 am on Monday, packing up to be home in time for work and school. We also went away every Easter and a month each Christmas holidays.

'Cooking and cooling were pretty basic – there was a metho stove and an ice chest that had a block of ice put into it twice a day. We had kerosene lamps for lighting, and in later years, a Portagas light. This of course limited the kind of cooking that was done, so we had a lot of barbecues and cold meat salads. Before eskies were on the market, Dad (who was a bit of an inventor) built a portable icebox for us to take to picnics. It was made of timber, lined with caneite and galvanised steel sheeting. It was very large and heavy but it did the job!

'Dad's wicked sense of humour was never too far away and our camping trips were fertile ground for his practical jokes. We were often the only people in the campground with a van and everyone else would be in tents. One time, Dad went to the bloke in the tent next door and told him that he had just heard on the radio that there was a huge storm coming and they had better batten down the hatches. (We didn't even have a radio.) The word went around the ground very quickly and Dad took great amusement from sitting back and watching everyone digging trenches around the tents and tying everything down.

'A favourite activity on our camping trips was prawning. We had a hand dragnet, which was allowed in those days. Mum's father made the dragnet. We would go out on the lake at night when the prawns were running and bring in a haul of small, sweet school prawns. The prawns were boiled in a 4 gallon drum over the fire. I can still taste the great prawn sandwiches made with fresh bakery bread and lashings of butter.

'We often went for drives in our A Model Ford and stopped by the side of the road for a picnic. Mum would bring date scones or cake in airtight tins. Dad would build a fire and boil a billy over it, with some gumleaves thrown in for flavour.

'I now treasure beyond words these memories of my dad, his skill at carpentry, his larrikin sense of humour, our family holidays and his adoration for Mum and us kids. He died when I was sixteen. I have missed him every day since. He remained the one and only love of Mum's life until she passed away last year aged ninety. At least I know they are together again.'

# 9 | Christmas *feast*

I love Christmas. I love the frantic lead-up, the last-minute panic, and the vast sense of relief come Christmas Eve – nothing more can be done but to enjoy the days ahead. Our Christmas traditions and rituals vary little from year to year.

On Christmas Eve, after Mass, our family has a roast dinner, followed by a drive around the streets to look at the Christmas lights. (Something we've meant to do every night for the past two weeks.) We get home and replace the dozens of decorations that have fallen off the Christmas tree since we left an hour earlier. We put out Santa's snacks and something for the reindeer. (We figure that Santa may be sick of Christmas cake by the time he gets to our place, so we give him a beer and some nuts.) We drape the stockings (read: huge pillowcases) on furniture around the lounge room.

After the boys are in bed, with visions of PlayStations dancing in their heads, Mick and I finally sit down with a drink, and exchange one gift. This is our moment to reflect, to be thankful, and to take a deep breath before Christmas Day arrives. It is the eye of the storm, the calm moment that I keep in my pocket and touch like a talisman whenever I need to over the coming days. It is, for me, the spiritual centre of Christmas, when my children are safe and sleeping, my house is quiet, and the true meaning of the day has a chance to settle into my heart.

Then there's the headlong rush into the main event – Christmas Day with my family, Boxing Day with Mick's, as it ever has been.

Here's Christmas. It is a whirlwind of love and laughter and wrapping paper and people and animals and noise. And food. Oh, my goodness, the food. Bowls of nuts and lollies and pretzels and chocolate-coated everything. The ham, the prawns, the salads and desserts (which no one can fit in but everyone eats anyway). And so it goes until we have all eaten ourselves to capacity several times over and need a couple of antacids and a lie-down.

This is Christmas, and it is good.

# Roast loin of pork with gravy

## serves 8–10

Preparation time: 30 minutes
Cooking time: 2½ hours

Roast pork is a traditional favourite for Christmas and my boys love it.
Whenever I roast pork I ask the butcher if he has any extra rind, and if he does,
I cook it separately. It ensures that everyone has as much crackling as they want!

2 kg rolled pork loin, boned
olive oil, for rubbing
1 tbs sea salt
rosemary sprigs, to serve

**Gravy**
1 cup (250 ml) white wine
2 cups (500 ml) liquid chicken stock
2 tbs plain flour
salt and white pepper, to taste

1   Preheat the oven to 220°C (200°C fan-forced). Use a small sharp knife or Stanley knife to
score the rind of the pork, and rub with oil. Massage the salt very thoroughly into the skin.
Place on a rack in a flame-proof baking dish with 1–2 cm water in the bottom.

2   Roast for 30 minutes, then reduce the temperature to 160°C (140°C fan-forced) and roast for
a further 1½ hours. Test the pork to make sure it is cooked by inserting a bamboo skewer into the
roast. The juices that come out should be clear, not dark pink, and the crackling should be crunchy.
Remove the pork from the baking dish and rest in a warm place for 20 minutes before slicing.

3   To make the gravy, pour the white wine and all but ½ cup (125 ml) stock into the baking dish.
Sit the dish over medium heat and stir with a spatula to remove all the tasty brown bits from
the bottom of the pan. Reduce until slightly thickened and tasty.

4   Mix the flour with the reserved chicken stock and stir well, ensuring there are no lumps.
Add the flour mixture to the pan a tablespoonful at a time, stirring well with a whisk after
each addition. Stir until the gravy boils and the flour is cooked, then add another tablespoonful.
Keep adding and stirring until the gravy thickens. Season to taste with salt and pepper.

5   Serve the pork with the gravy, apple sauce and crispy roast potatoes.

*Note*: For great crackling, make sure the rind is very dry before you begin.

# Apple sauce

## makes about 1½ cups

Preparation time: 5 minutes
Cooking time: 10 minutes

It just wouldn't be a pork roast without apple sauce.
This recipe is very straightforward. It can be done in the microwave if you prefer.

4 Granny Smith apples, peeled,
cored and chopped

caster sugar, to taste
pinch freshly grated nutmeg

1   Place the apples in a saucepan with ¼ cup (60 ml) water over medium heat and simmer until softened. Stir occasionally to ensure the apples don't stick to the pot. Taste and add sugar if the apples are too tart. I prefer a chunky apple sauce, but if you prefer yours smooth, process it in a blender or food processor.

2   Serve in a dish with a sprinkle of freshly grated nutmeg across the top.

# Crispy baked potatoes

serves 6–8 as an accompaniment (or 4–5 hungry teenagers!)

Preparation time: 15 minutes
Cooking time: 1 hour 15 minutes

There are as many methods of cooking baked potatoes as there are cooks. My mother-in-law Kathleen used to place the potatoes around the roasting joint of meat to mop up the flavour. The method I use involves boiling the potatoes first. The end result is beautiful, golden, crispy potatoes. No matter how many I make there are never leftovers.

2 kg potatoes, peeled      salt, to taste
vegetable oil, for baking

1  Preheat the oven to 200°C (180° fan-forced). Cut the potatoes in half, or in quarters if they're large – just make sure the pieces are evenly sized so they cook at the same time. Place the potatoes in a large pan of cold salted water and bring to the boil. Boil for around 15 minutes or until the cut edges are just starting to soften, and a knife or skewer goes easily into the potato. Don't cook any further than this or the potatoes will fall apart.

2  Drain the potatoes very well. It is critical that they are dry. If you are a more organised cook than I am, you could boil the potatoes the day before they are needed and keep them uncovered in the fridge. Meanwhile, put about 1 cm of vegetable oil into a roasting pan. Place the pan in the oven until the oil is hot.

3  Very carefully lower the potatoes into the hot oil. Gently turn them, so that the whole surface area of each potato has a coating of oil. Place the pan back in the oven and cook for about 1 hour, turning the potatoes once or twice, until they are crisp and golden brown. Drain on paper towels, and sprinkle with salt while still hot.

*Note*: For a variation, instead of plain salt make a flavoured salt by pounding rosemary, thyme or tarragon with rock salt in a mortar and pestle.

Christmas feast

# Baked ocean trout with seafood

## serves 6–8

Preparation time: 20 minutes
Cooking time: 45 minutes

This is one of Mum's favourite recipes for a dinner party. The wow factor is definitely there when it's presented and carved at the table. It is also a dramatic and gorgeous addition to the Christmas buffet.

1 whole fresh ocean trout (approx 2 kg), cleaned, head intact
12 green prawns, peeled and deveined
12 mussels, removed from shells
12 calamari rings

1 lemon, sliced
¼ cup (35 g) chopped pistachio kernels
juice of one lemon
sea salt and freshly ground black pepper

1 Preheat the oven to 180°C (160°C fan-forced). Make sure there are no scales left on the fish and that its insides have been cleaned thoroughly. Tear a sheet of non-stick baking paper and another of heavy foil, both about 30 cm longer than the fish. Lay the baking paper on the foil and place the fish in the centre.

2 Mix the prawns, mussels and calamari together and stuff them into the cavity of the fish, then place the lemon slices, slightly overlapping, on top of the fish. Sprinkle it with chopped pistachios and then pour over the lemon juice. Season generously.

3 Wrap the foil and baking paper around the fish, doubling the seams over several times to ensure no juices can escape. The main seam should be on top and run from the fish's head to its tail. Place the foil package in the oven and cook for 45 minutes. (For a larger trout, adjust the cooking time. A general rule is about 15 minutes per 500 g.)

4 Remove the fish from the oven and check that it is cooked. The eye should be white and the flesh just under done, as it will continue to cook while resting. Do not remove the foil or baking paper, just tear a little hole near the fish's head to check. If it is not ready, return the package to the oven for a further 10–15 minutes and then check again.

5 Place the package on a serving platter and allow to rest for 10 minutes. Mop up any excess juices with paper towel. To serve the fish whole at the table, neatly unwrap the foil and baking paper along the top seam. Carve the fish into segments, and carefully lift each slice with an egg flip onto each plate. The seafood stuffing is served to the side. When the top half of the fish is served, lift away the back bone and any other visible bones, exposing the bottom half, then serve the remaining fish.

# Henebery Boxing Day ham

serves the whole hungry Henebery clan

Preparation time: 15 minutes
Cooking time: 3 hours

In our family, Boxing Day is just as big a party as Christmas. We are so lucky that the two sides of our family celebrate Christmas over the two days, so we get to be with both sides every year. Boxing Day is a repeat performance of Christmas Day, but with more people and therefore more food. That's right, more food. Mick's mum's family, the Heneberys, are well known for their huge get-togethers and the copious amounts of food that are brought and cooked for every occasion. It is a family tradition to cook this ham on the barbecue, but it can just as easily be done in an oven, uncovered, at 160°C (140°C fan-forced) for 3 hours.

| | |
|---|---|
| 7 kg leg of ham | 1 tbs soy sauce |
| 250 g jar of marmalade | 2 tbs Dijon mustard |
| 1 cup (250 ml) fresh orange juice | 1 garlic clove, crushed |

1   Preheat a hooded barbecue to 160°C. Carefully remove the rind from the ham, but leave a good layer of fat intact. Score the fat in a diamond pattern, being careful not to cut through to the meat, or the fat will separate during cooking. In a few places, make a deep incision with a small-bladed knife.

2   Combine the marmalade, orange juice, soy sauce, mustard and garlic in a saucepan. Heat until the ingredients are warm and softened enough to mix well, but do not let them boil.

3   Using a pastry brush, baste the ham generously with the marinade, ensuring some of the marinade goes into the incisions.

4   Place the ham in a large baking dish and cook in the barbecue with the hood on for around 3 hours, basting it with the marinade several times during cooking.

*'The Dutch tend to celebrate things on the eve rather than the actual day. Because Dad was Dutch we would go to Midnight Mass, then go home and wait for him to come home from his shift at the post office. Then we would open presents.' – Marcus*

# Grandma's Christmas cake

## serves the multitudes

Preparation time: 20 minutes
Cooking time: 2 hours 40 minutes

Grandma was the queen of Christmas and reigned over it happily every year.
Her Christmas cake was legend among her family, friends and neighbours and continues
to be made every year by her daughters and granddaughters.

500 g unsalted butter
500 g sugar
8 eggs
finely grated zest and juice of 1 lemon
500 g currants
250 g raisins
60 g mixed peel

200 g glacé cherries, roughly chopped
1 tablespoon brandy
500 g plain flour
250 g self-raising flour
pinch salt
100 g blanched almonds

1   Preheat the oven to 200°C (180°C fan-forced). Grease a 24 cm square cake tin and line it with non-stick baking paper. Using electric beaters, beat the butter and sugar in a large bowl until creamy and pale. Add the eggs one at a time, beating after each addition.

2   Stir in the lemon zest and juice, fruit and brandy. Gently fold the flour and salt through. Spoon the mixture into the cake tin and smooth the surface. Arrange the blanched almonds in a pattern on the top.

3   Bake for 10 minutes, then reduce the heat to 150°C (130°C fan-forced) and bake for a further 30 minutes. Reduce the heat again to 120°C (100°C fan-forced) and cook for another 2 hours or until a skewer inserted comes out clean.

*For about the past five years, I have organised a street Christmas party.
Everybody brings food to share and we have a barbecue. I was quite nervous about it
the first year. We don't live in each others' pockets here and I wasn't sure how the idea
would be received. But everyone insisted that it was beautiful, so it's now a standing
date on everyone's calendar. We get together and have a good laugh,
and it wouldn't be Christmas without it.' – Vickie*

For as long as I can remember, my Great-Aunty Joyce made this plum pudding for Christmas, filled with old coins. Even though I was never a big fan of the pudding, I always loved the custard – and the race to find the money. I also loved the theatre of it. It arrived at the table huge and round and burning with a blue brandy flame.

Before Aunty Joyce, my great-grandmother used to make it. She would make two, one for Christmas and one for New Year. Family legend has it that one year she was busy giving birth at home during dessert time, so she asked her brother to serve the pudding. As there were four people present, he cut the pudding into four and they ate the lot in one go.

You can use the recipe overleaf to make two puddings for your crowd, or give one away. If you want to make one large pudding, double the cooking time. Pudding cloths can be purchased at a fabric store, or use unbleached calico. You will need two cloths, about 60 cm square.

# Great-Grandma's plum pudding
## makes 2 crowd-feeding plum puddings

Preparation time: 2 months
Cooking time: 4 hours + 1½ hours reheating time

375 g butter
1¼ cups (250 g) brown sugar
4 eggs
250 g fresh white breadcrumbs
1 kg raisins
2 cups (300 g) currants

1⅔ cups (250 g) plain flour
½ tsp bicarb soda
2 tbs mixed spice
1 tbs nutmeg
100 ml brandy
½ cup (125 ml) brandy, to serve

1 Using electric beaters, beat the butter and sugar until light and creamy. Add the eggs one at a time, beating well after each addition, then stir in the breadcrumbs. Next add the fruit and sifted dry ingredients and stir in the brandy.

2 Drop the pudding cloths into a saucepan of boiling water and boil for a couple of minutes. Remove from the pan, cool, then wring out the excess water. Thickly coat one side of each cloth with flour and put them into colanders, floured side up.

3 Divide the pudding mixture in half, and place one half in the centre of each cloth. Gather up the edges, being careful not to create too many creases. Leave about 1 cm at the top for the pudding to swell during cooking, and tie very tightly with string.

4 Fill two very large pots with water and place a plate upside down in the base of each one. (The plate will stop the pudding from sticking to the pot and boiling dry.) Bring to the boil and plunge the puddings in. Bring back to a gentle simmer and simmer for 4 hours. Remove the puddings from the pot and hang them in a cool place, still in their cloths. Hang them for several days until they dry out enough to hold their shape, then place them in the fridge or freezer, still in their cloths. If freezing, defrost them the day before eating.

5 On Christmas day, re-heat by simmering in a large pot of water for about 1½ hours. Take out and place into a colander. Cut the string and turn back the cloth. Put a large serving platter on top, and turn right way up. Pour warmed brandy over the pudding and set it alight. Carry to the table with much pomp and circumstance – this thing was weeks in the making!

'On Christmas Eve, Mum and Dad always had the neighbours in for a party. We would try to get to Mass before the party, because by Midnight Mass nobody was really fit to drive. On Christmas morning we always had to wait for each other to wake up. Then we would go downstairs and see if Santa had been. Mum would hand out the presents, then we'd head to Grandma and Grandpa's for lunch. There were loads of people, tons of food, pennies in the pudding, and gifts for everybody.' – Rebecca

'The lead-up to Christmas is the time of year that the children love most. We light the Advent candle on the appropriate nights, and we make every meal festive.' – Vickie

'We have two traditions – one old and one new. The old tradition is a full roast turkey dinner on Christmas Day. We make everything from scratch, including the stuffing, which is so plentiful it doesn't all fit in the bird. We came from England so this harks back to a winter Christmas. It's much better now that Mum and Dad have air conditioning! Our new tradition is that every year Adam heads down to the Sydney fish markets and buys mountains of seafood. We then have a giant seafood barbecue with cocktails.' – Steph

# Christmas ice-cream pudding

## serves 8

........................................................................................

Preparation time: 20 minutes
Chill time: 8 hours minimum

Here is a dessert that looks like a Christmas pudding, but is made of chocolate
ice-cream, especially for our hot climate. You can experiment with the lollies and
chocolates that you put into the pudding.

2 litres good-quality chocolate ice-cream
100 g nougat, chopped
140 g packet of Maltesers
1 cup (60 g) mini marshmallows
12 pieces (120 g) Violet Crumble,
roughly chopped

½ cup (90 g) white chocolate chips
100 g Turkish delight, roughly chopped
150 g good quality white cooking
chocolate, chopped

1   Spray a 2 litre pudding basin or glass mixing bowl with cooking spray. Lay cling wrap in the
bowl, keeping it as smooth as possible. Leave plenty of cling wrap hanging over the edges.

2   Leave the ice-cream out of the freezer to soften slightly. It should not be too liquid, or the lollies
will all end up at the bottom of the basin. Carefully stir all the lollies into the ice-cream. Spoon
into the prepared basin. Smooth the surface and cover with the overhanging plastic wrap. Freeze
for at least 8 hours, or until very firm. (Overnight is best.)

3   Melt the white chocolate in a glass bowl over a pan of barely simmering water, making sure
the bowl doesn't touch the water. As the chocolate starts to soften, stir it well with a metal spoon
until smooth. Set aside to cool and thicken to the consistency of thick cream. The time will vary
depending on the room temperature, but don't put it in the fridge, as it will set too hard.

4   To serve, turn the pudding onto a chilled plate. Remove the cling wrap and spoon the melted
chocolate on top, allowing it to run down the sides a little bit. Place back in the freezer for
5 minutes, until the chocolate sets. Decorate the top with a holly sprig, or with Turkish delight and
fairy floss, or choc-coated nuts – be as creative as you like. Cut the pudding into wedges with
a very sharp knife dipped in hot water and clean it after each cut. Put any leftovers straight
back into the freezer!

# Huge celebration pavlova

## makes one very big pavlova

Preparation time: 20 minutes
Cooking time: 1 hour 10 minutes

Who doesn't love a pavlova? It's the quintessential Australian dessert. It speaks to me of summer, and I decorate mine with whatever fruits are in season. I have included this in the Christmas chapter because it's a perfect Christmas Day dessert – it can be made beforehand, assembled in moments and isn't too rich or heavy after the huge lunch everybody has no doubt enjoyed.

6 eggwhites
¼ tsp salt
1⅔ cups (370 g) caster sugar
1 tbs cornflour
1 tsp white vinegar

1 tsp vanilla extract
600 ml cream, whipped
fresh seasonal fruit (mango slices, strawberries, passionfruit, raspberries . . .)

1   Preheat oven to 170°C (150°C fan-forced). Grease a 38 × 25 cm baking tray and line it with non-stick baking paper. Beat the eggwhites and salt in an electric mixer until soft peaks appear. Begin adding the caster sugar a little at a time, until it is all incorporated. Continue to mix until the eggwhites form stiff, glossy peaks.

2   Gently fold in the cornflour, vinegar and vanilla, being careful not to knock the air out of the mixture. Spread the mixture onto the baking tray, leaving a 2 cm space around the edges.

3   Bake for 30 minutes, then reduce the temperature to 140°C (120°C fan-forced) and bake for a further 40 minutes. Turn the oven off and prop the door open an inch. Allow the pavlova to cool in the oven. When it is completely cool, top with whipped cream and fruit to serve.

*'Our son Greg is twenty-seven and he still sleeps under the Christmas tree to try and catch Santa in the act. He hasn't caught him yet!' – Gabrielle*

# 10 | Our family table

When I asked the people around me for their food memories, it opened up a dialogue that drew in dozens of people, and the most wonderful things came about. That is the nature of food, though – even the discussion of it brings people together.

Everyone has a favourite food memory from childhood – and from more recent years. Everyone remembers some disaster or some perfectly special occasion.

It is with great pleasure that I hand the baton to you.

In the conversations you have with your family and friends, I hope you uncover some culinary treasures as I did, and can take a walk down memory lane. I hope that when you have filled this chapter up, you will get yourself a beautiful notebook and keep going. So much history is lost because it is not recorded. I hope that you will write down as much as you can, for yourself and for future generations.

I hope you collect recipes, memories, thoughts, anecdotes, photographs, drawings. They are all a part of the story.

# PASSIONFRIUT SHORT-CAKE

PASTRY:-

4 ozs. butter
8 ozs. S.R. flour
4 ozs. sugar
1 egg

METHOD:-

With your fingers, rub the butter into the sifted flour till it is like breadcrumbs.

Add the sugar and mix together.

Beat the egg and add it to the mixture. It makes a dry crumbly mixture.

Grease and flour an 8" sandwich ...

Passionfruit shortbread
250 grms butter
½ cup castor sugar
1 egg yolk
pulp 3 passionfruit
2 cups plain flour
½ cup corn flour
1½ teaspoons baking powd
mod. oven
Cream 1st four ingredients
fold in flours.
Cream
1 tablespoon butter
1½ " passion pulp
1 cup icing sugar
shopping is
and friendly atmo
happy to help you to selec
of wishing you the Compliment
O. J. Willia

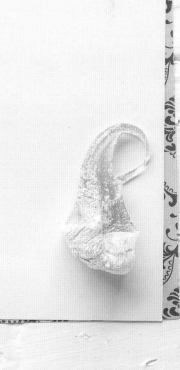

*Above left: Me on my second birthday with
a Humpty Dumpty cake*

*Above right: My sister, Debbie, on her first
birthday, with a teddy bear cake*

# Acknowledgements

It has been amazing to discover just how many people are involved in bringing a book into being. I owe thanks to so many people for their talent and dedication to this project, and for making it possible.

Thanks to all the wonderful people at Random House Australia, including Nikki Christer, Nikla Martin and especially my editor, Elizabeth Cowell.

Thank you to living legend Margaret Fulton, who wrote the foreword. Meeting my hero and finding her to be as exceptional a human being in real life as I had always imagined is a dream come true. Thank you, Margaret.

To the team who tested the recipes and photographed the food – thank you for being such a wonderful group of people to work with. Food testers extraordinaire Tracy Rutherford and Kellie Thomas, thanks for all your hard work and advice (and for feeding the neighbourhood in the process). Nick Eade, thanks for cooking the food so beautifully for the photography. Janelle Bloom, stylist, brilliant cook and all-round wonderful human being, thank you. Steve Brown, your photography is just breathtaking and you are a pleasure to work with. Laura Jenkins, thank you for helping so willingly. Thanks to Kellie Gray and Stephanie Tetu for your hair-taming abilities. To Jay Ryves, thank you for the gorgeous internal design and the long, long hours you put in, and to Mary Callahan, thank you for the elegant cover.

I would also like to express my gratitude to those who opened their homes for the photography – Tracy and Richo, Debbie and Mark.

Of course I would not even be in this position if it weren't for the amazing experience of being on the first series of *MasterChef Australia*. I offer heartfelt thanks to Channel Ten for taking a chance on the production. And I owe a huge debt of gratitude to FremantleMedia Australia for creating such a positive program. From the very top of the management tree right through to every single producer, director and crew member that I had the good fortune to work with, thanks to each one of you.

Thank you to Gary Mehigan, George Calombaris and Matt Preston for having the faith to put me through in the first place, and for fuelling my desire to learn and improve along the way. Thanks to Sarah Wilson for kindness and wisdom when it was so needed. Thanks to all the chefs who came onto the series and so generously shared with us. I will always be grateful to each of you.

Thanks also to Lisa Sullivan and Forum 5 for everything you've done for me.

To walk away from my whole life for over four months took the support of many wonderful people, and they all played a role in the outcome. Thanks to my parents, Marlene and Tony Hunt, who came and helped out every week while I was away, and my sister, Debbie Hunt, who jumped right in the deep end at the office. You not only offered practical support but great encouragement and belief as well, as you have all my life. Thanks to all our extended family who offered support both moral and practical. Thank you to our faithful friends and community who all supported Mick and the boys, and wrote to me and helped keep me going. We are very lucky people. Thanks also to the team at Loyal I.T. Solutions – you have been so gracious about my rapid exit from the company and I miss you every day.

Of course my greatest thanks must go to the people who made the biggest sacrifice for me to be gone for such a long time. My stunning sons, Joe, Tom and Paddy, never once asked me to come home, and gave me nothing but encouragement even as they were crying down the phone line. My gratitude for your presence in my life cannot be expressed. Thank you for going through all of it and thank you for being so understanding even now, when things are still a crazy whirlwind. Your resilience, unselfishness and your loving hearts make me so very proud of you.

Mick – well, there just aren't the words to thank you for what you went through, the burden you shouldered and the love and support you give me. Only you and I will ever really know what that time was like. Thank you for being my life partner, my best mate and my heart. To you and to our boys, I dedicate this book and I dedicate my life.

*Grandpa's birthday picnic*

# Index

*My mum, Marlene, with a dolly cake*

*Eighth birthday spread*

An Ebury Press book
Published by Random House Australia Pty Ltd

Level 3, 100 Pacific Highway, North Sydney NSW 2060
www.randomhouse.com.au

First published by Ebury Press in 2010

Addresses for companies within the Random House Group
can be found at www.randomhouse.com.au/offices

National Library of Australia
Cataloguing-in-Publication Entry
Author: Goodwin, Julie.
Title: Our Family Table / Julie Goodwin.
ISBN: 978 1 74166 968 8 (pbk.)
Subjects: Cookery.
Dewey Number: 641.5

Cover design by Mary Callahan Design
Internal design and typesetting by Jay Ryves, Future Classic
Recipe testing and editing by Tracy Rutherford and Kellie Thomas
Food styling by Janelle Bloom
Photography by Steve Brown
Index by Jon Jermey
Printed and bound by 1010 Printing International Ltd. Printed in China.

The publishers would like to thank Waterford Crystal, Wedgwood, Sheldon & Hammond, Village Living Avalon, Major & Tom, Mud Australia, Ici et Là and Autograph for the gorgeous props, clothes and fabrics used throughout this book.

Random House Australia uses papers that are natural, renewable and recyclable products and made from wood grown in sustainable forests. The logging and manufacturing processes are expected to conform to the environmental regulations of the country of origin.

10 9 8 7 6 5

custard consistency. Add dissolved gelatine, stirring
until mixture cools. Whisk 2 egg whites add to
stiff froth, add ¼ cup sugar Combine the mixture
add to pie shell and chill before cutting.

## Marys' Christmas cake

Ingredients:- ½ lb. butter ¼ lb. brown & ¼ lb. white sugar
10 ozs. plain flour ½ teaspoon soda, ½ cup
sherry 2 teaspoons spice, 1 lb. raisins ½ lb.
sultanas, ½ lb. currants ¼ cherries ¼ figs
¼ lb. peel 5 eggs ½ milk, pinch salt.

Method :- Beat butter & sugar to a cream then
add beaten eggs, dry ingredients sifted, then
fruit. Mix then add enough milk to make the
mixture thin. Bake first 20 minutes at 400 &
turn to 300 for 10 minutes then 250 or 200 till
cooked. About 4 hours in all

## Barley Flakes Plum Pudding

Soak one cup of barley flakes in milk for about
hour. Then mix with one large cup of breadcrumbs